# The Work
of the People

# The Vital Worship, Healthy Congregations Series

John D. Witvliet, Series Editor

Published by the Alban Institute in cooperation with the
Calvin Institute of Christian Worship

## BOOKS IN THE SERIES

C. Michael Hawn
*One Bread, One Body:*
*Exploring Cultural Diversity in Worship*

Norma deWaal Malefyt and Howard Vanderwell
*Designing Worship Together:*
*Models and Strategies for Worship Planning*

Craig A. Satterlee
*When God Speaks through Change:*
*Preaching in Times of Congregational Transition*

Peter Bush and Christine O'Reilly
*Where 20 or 30 Are Gathered:*
*Leading Worship in the Small Church*

Robert P. Glick
*With All Thy Mind:*
*Worship That Honors the Way God Made Us*

Kathleen S. Smith
*Stilling the Storm:*
*Worship and Congregational Leadership in Difficult Times*

Marlea Gilbert, Christopher Grundy, Eric T. Myers, and Stephanie Perdew
*The Work of the People:*
*What We Do in Worship and Why*

# The Work of the People

## What We Do in Worship and Why

Marlea Gilbert &
Christopher Grundy, Eric T. Myers, and Stephanie Perdew

THE
ALBAN
INSTITUTE

Herndon, Virginia
www.alban.org

The Alban Institute
2121 Cooperative Way, Suite 100
Herndon, VA 20171

Unless otherwise noted, all Scripture quotations are from the New Revised Standard Version of the Bible, copyright © 1989, Division of Christian Education of the National Council of the Churches of Christ in the United States of America, and are used by permission.

Cover design by Wendy Ronga, Hampton Design Group.

Library of Congress Cataloging-in-Publication Data

The work of the people : what we do in worship and why / Marlea Gilbert ... [et al.] ; foreword by Ruth Duck.
    p. cm. -- (The vital worship, healthy congregations series)
Includes bibliographical references.
ISBN-13: 978-1-56699-337-1
ISBN-10: 1-56699-337-7
1. Protestant churches--Liturgy. I. Gilbert, Marlea.
BV176.3.W67 2007
264--dc22

                                        2006100214

    11   10   09   08   07      VG      1   2   3   4   5

Dedicated to Gabe Huck, publisher, advocate, and teacher, whose passion for liturgy is our inspiration.

# Contents

# Editor's Foreword

## Healthy Congregations

Christianity is a "first-person plural" religion, where communal worship, service, fellowship, and learning are indispensable for grounding and forming individual faith. The strength of Christianity in North America depends on the presence of healthy, spiritually nourishing, well-functioning congregations. Congregations are the cradle of Christian faith, the communities in which children of all ages are supported, encouraged, and formed for lives of service. Congregations are the habitat in which the practices of the Christian life can flourish.

As living organisms, congregations are by definition in a constant state of change. Whether the changes are in membership, pastoral leadership, lay leadership, the needs of the community, or the broader culture, a crucial mark of healthy congregations is their ability to deal creatively and positively with change. The fast pace of change in contemporary culture, with its bias toward, not against, change only makes the challenge of negotiating change all the more pressing for congregations.

## Vital Worship

At the center of many discussions about change in churches today is the topic of worship. This is not surprising, for worship is at the center of congregational life. To "go to church" means, for most members of congregations, "to go to worship." In *How*

*Do We Worship?*, Mark Chaves begins his analysis with the simple assertion, "Worship is the most central and public activity engaged in by American religious congregations" (Alban Institute, 1999, p. 1). Worship styles are one of the most significant reasons that people choose to join a given congregation. Correspondingly, they are central to the identity of most congregations.

Worship is also central on a much deeper level. Worship is the locus of what several Christian traditions identify as the nourishing center of congregational life: preaching, common prayer, and the celebration of ordinances or sacraments. Significantly, what many traditions elevate to the status of "the means of grace" or even the "marks of the church" are essentially liturgical actions. Worship is central, most significantly, for theological reasons. Worship both reflects and shapes a community's faith. It expresses a congregation's view of God and enacts a congregation's relationship with God and each other.

We can identify several specific factors that contribute to spiritually vital worship and thereby strengthen congregational life.

- Congregations, and the leaders that serve them, need a shared vision for worship that is grounded in more than personal aesthetic tastes. This vision must draw on the deep theological resources of Scripture, the Christian tradition, and the unique history of the congregation.
- Congregational worship should be integrated with the whole life of the congregation. It can serve as the "source and summit" from which all the practices of the Christian life flow. Worship both reflects and shapes the life of the church in education, pastoral care, community service, fellowship, justice, hospitality, and every other aspect of church life.

- The best worship practices feature not only good worship "content," such as discerning sermons, honest prayers, creative artistic contributions, celebrative and meaningful rituals for baptism and the Lord's Supper. They also arise out of good process, involving meaningful contributions from participants, thoughtful leadership, honest evaluation, and healthy communication among leaders.

## Vital Worship, Healthy Congregations Series

The Vital Worship, Healthy Congregations Series is designed to reflect the kind of vibrant, creative energy and patient reflection that will promote worship that is both relevant and profound. It is designed to invite congregations to rediscover a common vision for worship, to sense how worship is related to all aspects of congregational life, and to imagine better ways of preparing both better "content" and better "process" related to the worship life of their own congregations.

It is important to note that strengthening congregational life through worship renewal is a delicate and challenging task precisely because of the uniqueness of each congregation. This book series is not designed to represent a single denomination, Christian tradition, or type of congregation. Nor is it designed to serve as arbiter of theological disputes about worship. Books in the series will note the significance of theological claims about worship, but they may, in fact, represent quite different theological visions from each other, or from our work at the Calvin Institute of Christian Worship. That is, the series is designed to call attention to instructive examples of congregational life and to explore these examples in ways that allow readers in very different communities to compare and contrast these examples with their own practice.

The models described in any given book may for some readers be instructive as examples to follow. For others, a given example may remind them of something they are already doing well, or something they will choose not to follow because of theological commitments or community history.

In the first volume in our series, *One Bread, One Body: Exploring Cultural Diversity in Worship,* Michael Hawn poses the poignant question "is there room for my neighbor at the table?" and explores what four multicultural congregations have to teach us about hospitality and the virtues of cross-cultural worship. His work helps us step back and reflect on the core identity of our congregations.

In our second volume, *Designing Worship Together: Models and Strategies for Worship Planning,* Norma deWaal Malefyt and Howard Vanderwell enter the trenches of weekly congregational life. They give us helpful insights into the process of how services are planned and led. It is hard to overstate the significance of this topic. For without a thoughtful, discerning, collaborative worship planning process, all manner of worship books, conferences, and renewal programs are likely either to make no inroads into the life of a given congregation or, when they do, to damage rather than renew congregational life.

In the third volume, *When God Speaks through Change: Preaching in Times of Congregational Transition,* Craig Satterlee addresses the question of how worship (and particularly preaching) might best respond to times of significant congregational transition. The vast majority of published perspectives and resources for preaching and worship unwittingly assume a level of constancy in congregational life, taking for granted that the congregation will have the resources (emotional and otherwise) to absorb some significant new message or practice. However, on any given Sunday, a strikingly large number of churches are simply trying to cope with a significant transition in community life or leadership. These transitions do limit what preachers and worship leaders can do on Sunday, but they also present unparalleled opportunities for the reception of the gospel. For congregations in transition, this book provides a useful and necessary frame for viewing almost all other advice and resources about what should happen in public worship.

In the fourth volume, *Where 20 or 30 Are Gathered: Leading Worship in the Small Church,* Peter Bush and Christine O'Reilly probe a topic that is instructive not only for small congregations, but also for large ones. When representatives of small congregations attend worship conferences or read books about worship they are frequently confronted with practices and resources that are entirely impractical for their purposes, requiring time and money that simply aren't available. Yet, as Bush and O'Reilly demonstrate, "small" certainly does not mean "deficient." In fact, smaller congregations have the potential to achieve participation, flexibility, and intimacy that larger congregations find much harder to achieve. In the upside-down world of the kingdom of God, could it be that those of us from larger congregations should be attending conferences in smaller congregations, rather than just the other way around?

In our fifth volume, *With All Thy Mind: Worship That Honors the Way God Made Us,* Robert Glick turns our attention to the people who gather for worship. As alert pastors know so well, when worshipers assemble they bring with them remarkable differences in aptitude, temperament, and preferences. For leaders who eagerly desire that their congregations participate in worship in knowing and engaged ways, coming to terms with this diversity is essential. It is otherwise too tempting for preachers to prepare sermons and musicians to prepare music for people who are just like themselves. Recent writers have given us several ways to understand the diversity of persons

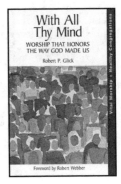

who worship: personality type indicators, theories of multiple intelligences, and right-brain/left-brain differences. Glick works with the latter approach to help us understand that some differences among us can't be resolved by simply asserting our own point of view more loudly.

By now, readers can sense an important pattern in this series. Our goal is to probe several pastoral realities that many books about worship often ignore. This is especially true of this volume, Kathy Smith's *Stilling the Storm: Worship and Congregational Leadership in Difficult Times*. Moments of crisis, transition, and conflict are those in which congregations most need well-grounded, vibrant worship practices. Yet they are precisely the times in which the leadership capacity of many congregations is most threatened.

This is particularly true when worship itself is the source of conflict. We feel out of balance precisely when we most need pastoral poise. Yet worship experts in many traditions continue to offer advice mostly for periods of stability, growth, and resource expansion, ignoring the simple fact that pastoral ministry is more often practiced in the messiness of uncertain and challenging circumstances. Rev. Smith begins to fill this lacuna here, drawing on her years of experience as pastor, teacher, administrator, and leader. As she suggests, it is during times of uncertainty that we learn the habits of trust, vulnerability, and patience that are so fundamental to a vital Christian life and, ultimately, to worship itself. Indeed, in the surprising upside-down world of the gospel, worship is yet one more place where to lose our life is to find it. May this book not only instruct many of us to prepare for difficult times, but also buoy those who are caught in the middle of them.

*The Work of the People: What We Do in Worship and Why* turns our attention from those who lead congregations to all worshipers. In our work at the Calvin Institute of Christian Worship, we have been happily surprised at the number of pastors in many denominations who describe the eagerness of many lay people to better understand worship. As one pastor commented, "for some of my people, attending worship is like going to a baseball game without knowing the rules. They are interested in it, but simply can't get excited about it, and they certainly can't deeply appreciate it." Many of these pastors testify that excellent education about the shape and purpose of worship is one of the most promising approaches for spurring worship renewal. *The Work of the People* is designed precisely to contribute to this educational and formational process. The volume is especially strong at linking theological vision with concrete practices. This remedies the frequent problem of treatments of worship on the one hand that are theologically robust but disconnected from actual practice and those on the other that focus entirely on the mechanics of liturgy but lack theological vision.

By promoting encounters with instructive examples from various parts of the body of Christ, we pray that these volumes will help leaders make good judgments about worship in their congregations and that, by the power of God's Spirit, these congregations will flourish.

John D. Witvliet
Calvin Institute of Christian Worship

# Foreword

One of the best kept secrets about worship in the
North American context is that while style matters,
care matters even more. Preparing and leading worship with prayerful attention both to practical details
and to theological meanings will bear fruit in worship that energizes the spiritual and communal life
of congregations. God is in the details, from vesting
the space to preparing readers to considering whether
our methods of sharing bread and cup are consistent
with our beliefs about the sacrament of the table. Attention to details is not only a matter of rules or ru-
brics (which often do offer ritual wisdom) but also of
Christians lavishing their love and their best human
gifts so that the whole people of God may participate
in worship with heart, mind, and soul.

With *The Work of the People*, the secret is out.
The authors show how and why to prepare worship
with loving care. I am delighted at its publication, and
not only because Marlea Gilbert, Christopher Grundy, Eric Myers, and Stephanie Perdew are among the
first students and graduates of our Liturgical Studies
Ph.D. program at Garrett-Evangelical Theological
Seminary. I expect that this book will contribute to
the renewal of worship by serving as a resource both
for students preparing for ministry in local congregations and for local church members and committees
seeking to revitalize worship.

I have been assigning the manuscript as required
reading for basic worship courses. I do not know of
any book that provides more helpful information

about how to lead worship graciously or that raises basic theological issues about worship more concisely. I expect that having read this book, someone leading or planning worship for the first time would do so much more effectively.

Yet the book also has much to offer seasoned liturgical practitioners. The methods it encourages are more like slow home cooking than fast food. The authors offer practices and patterns that, when followed over time, will nourish churches in wholesome, heartfelt worship. Local church leaders (laity, pastors, educators, and musicians) can read it together as a springboard for discussion of what Christian worship means and how their congregation's worship can grow in faithfulness and vitality.

The book moves through preparation, gathering, attending to the word, praying for the world, celebrating Eucharist, and sending forth—and everything in between. This framework provides opportunity for the authors to comment on everything from the placement of announcements to why they (in accord with Luther, Calvin, and Wesley) believe Holy Communion should be a weekly part of Sunday worship. They are gracious and wise in their recommendations. Without being pedantic or antiquarian, they bring their considerable knowledge of the history and theology of worship to bear on the issues they address. Not championing a particular style of worship or music, they offer thoughtful insights toward engaging children and young people in worship and calling forth energized participation from Christians of all age groups.

Vitality in worship is a quality that cannot be measured by numbers or statistics or served up through styles, rules, or gimmicks. The authors point the way toward vital worship: deep love of God, openhanded hospitality toward all people, loving attention to details in planning and leadership, and vibrant faith that draws others into faith and discipleship.

Read this small book slowly and ponder it, for much deep thought underlies its simple expression.

Ruth Duck
Professor of Worship
Garrett-Evangelical Theological Seminary
Evanston, Illinois

# Preface

This project began as a class assignment in a Ph.D. seminar taught by Gabe Huck. Gabe spent much of his publishing career helping Roman Catholic congregations understand and participate fully in the revised liturgy developed as a result of Vatican II. The four authors of this book, three from the United Church of Christ and one Presbyterian (U.S.A.), found inspiration in Gabe's passion and pastoral approach, but we wondered how we could apply his approach to our own very different settings. The liturgies in our denominational materials have much in common with the Roman Catholic ones, but there is no authority requiring adherence to those liturgies. Congregational freedom of worship is a firm principle in our churches. Rather than prepare independent papers on unrelated subjects, we decided to work together on a single document that might help congregations in our own denominations and in others to better understand the intent of the liturgies created in the last two or three decades of the 20th century and appropriate the patterns and purposes into their weekly worship.

The original document we boldly titled *Vital Protestant Worship: A Letter to Churches*. Each of us took a section of the book. We discussed and agreed upon the principles to be presented in the introduction, and Marlea undertook that and the Sending as her task. Stephanie wrote about the Gathering, Eric had the chapter on the Word, and Christopher prepared the chapter on Prayer and Sacrament. We each included some sidebars with additional information. After the class was over, we made some adjustments to remove overlaps and to smooth transitions. In another class, Marlea prepared a study guide to accompany the text. This photocopied document has been used in worship classes taught by Christopher and by Ruth Duck and in a small number of congregations.

The original team is now scattered. Eric, Christopher, and Marlea finished their Ph.D. programs and graduated in May 2006. Eric and his family moved east, where Eric became pastor of Fredrick Presbyterian Church in Fredrick, Maryland. Christopher teaches at Eden Theological Seminary in St. Louis, Missouri and raises his family there. Stephanie started her program a year or so after the rest and is working on her dissertation as she continues to serve as pastor to First Congregational UCC in Wilmette, Illinois. Marlea is teaching part-time at Garrett-Evangelical Theological Seminary. She became the reviser of the main text and coordinator of the project. Christopher located and prepared most of the sidebars and callouts. Stephanie and Eric prepared the comprehensive chart and annotated bibliography of denominational worship resources in the appendix.

By using the book in her classroom, Ruth Duck affirmed its value and convinced us to seek publication. With the insightful assistance of our editor at Alban, Beth Ann Gaede, and the encouragement of the Calvin series editor, John Witvliet, the material has been broadened to address the needs of a wide variety of denominations and worship styles and more directly focused on its primary audience, members of congregations who want to better understand worship. We are grateful to the Alban Institute team and to our families and friends who have made room for this project in our lives.

Marlea Gilbert
October 2006
Baraboo, Wisconsin

Introduction

# Approaching Worship
## *Roots and Principles*

St. Peter's Church is a mainline congregation in an established suburb with a traditional worship service. It has been slowly losing members for several years. Nearby River of Life, a new, independent evangelical congregation, is growing. Three members of St. Peter's have visited a worship service at River of Life; they report that it uses a style of music and worship different from that of their own congregation; they wonder whether St. Peter's should try something similar. The debate at the worship committee is heated.

"What about our traditions?" one member asks.

"We haven't really tried the worship forms in the new hymnal and book of worship," says the pastor.

Peace Church has new members who come from a variety of denominations and faith traditions. Each wants to know why Peace does what it does in Sunday worship. They wonder: what is the difference whether we say a prayer of confession or a prayer of invocation? Just saying "This is the way we've always done it" is not enough.

Like many other congregations, St. Peter's and Peace use one of the generation of denominational hymnals published since 1980, whose orders of worship are shaped by the liturgical renewal movement. To some churches, the new orders seem too formal, or they bring in elements that longtime members associate with the Roman Catholic Church. Others feel as though they are losing some of the old familiar responses. How is a congregation to decide what the right form of worship is and why the worship patterns are changing? Why is the worship service structured the way it is?

# Our Purpose

Situations like those described above are common in congregations large and small, in various denominations, and in cities, suburbs, small towns, and rural areas. Our intent in writing this book and study guide is to help you, both laity and clergy, to revitalize or further strengthen worship in your congregation. We hope to help you to learn more about worship: to think about the structure of worship, the actions and words we use, and the environment in which worship takes place. We want to help you make the best use of available worship resources and to make the best choices about how you will worship together, while being respectful of local tradition, of the traditions and practices of the church as a whole, and being led by the Spirit in praise and worship of the God of all creation. In other words, we hope to help you think about what we do in worship and why. With that goal in mind, we offer this guide to aid study groups, worship committees, altar guilds, pastors, church musicians, and others with a special interest in worship.

Throughout the 20th century, and coming to full expression in the past 20 years, a liturgical renewal movement has grown up among scholars and church leaders who have studied the worship patterns of the early church in the context of contemporary theology. The result is a remarkable ecumenical consensus about the shape and content of worship that has influenced the writers of our hymnals and books of worship across a wide spectrum of denominations. Worship services following this consensus share a similar pattern of Scripture readings and a similar worship order. We hope to help you explore and apply some of the fruit of that liturgical renewal.

The authors of this book come from mainline denominations in the Reformed and free church traditions, those with roots in the Protestant Reformation of the 16th century and especially followers of John Calvin and Ulrich Zwingli. Today these denominations include Congregationalist and United Church of Christ, Presbyterian, and Christian Reformed congregations, plus those in Wesleyan (Methodist) traditions, Christian Church (Disciples of Christ) congregations and others that arose on or were shaped by life on the American frontier. Those in the Anglican tradition share a similar origin but have developed somewhat differently since the 18th century. Since the liturgical renewal movement and the ecumenical councils of the 1960s, these denominations have come to realize how much we share with Lutheran, Roman Catholic, and Orthodox sisters and brothers in Christ. As doctoral students in seminary, we have read and have been shaped by thinkers from a broad spectrum of the church, and we draw upon that breadth in this book. We believe that what we present here will have relevance for people in these and other Christian settings.

We believe that every congregation has the potential to worship in a way that is vital to the lives of those who participate: worship of spiritual depth that encourages the growth in faith of its participants, reaches out to and welcomes new participants into faith, and sends people out as the Body of Christ to transform the world. We also believe that many of the resources needed for vital worship are already on the shelves and in the hands of the people within many congregations. It is our hope that you will share our enthusiasm for the current and emerging denominational resources, as well as others that are available, and that you will find ways to make them part of your

> We believe that every congregation has the potential to worship in a way that is vital to the lives of those who participate.

regular worship. We also hope to offers tools to evaluate other resources so that all elements work together for the glory of God.

# The Roots of Our Worship

The last three decades of the 20th century in particular produced dramatic changes in the worship books of most mainline Protestant denominations. Even earlier, thinkers and leaders of many backgrounds were beginning to realize that current worship patterns were based on historical forces and conflicts that had shaped worship through the centuries but were no longer meaningful. Heightened by the discovery and translation early in the century of some early Christian writings, the most important being the Didache and the *Apostolic Tradition* of Hypolytus, a widespread interest arose among liturgical scholars in looking back to our roots, to the patterns of the early church, to see what might have been lost or buried that could be of value for worship today. The work of the Reformers was reexamined too; their worship practices and scriptural and theological insights contributed to the renewal.

Part of the liturgical renewal movement was a move toward greater *enculturation* of the liturgy, including the use of local music, art, and other cultural

As you explore some of the changes from previous practice found in your denominational worship books, it may be helpful to look back at some of the sources of "the way we've always done it" to see how relatively recent those ways are. A good starting place for such historical exploration is James White's *Protestant Worship: Traditions in Transition.*[1] For example, White traces the influence of frontier camp meetings on the worship order of many Protestant denominations. He also explores the influence of a mid-20th century reaction to that more casual style, one that reemphasized more elaborate buildings, large pipe organs, and robed choirs.

aspects in worship. As the movement came to fruition in the 1960s and 1970s, it was accompanied by an enthusiasm, which burst forth strongly in the Roman Catholic Church but spread widely, for using popular styles of music and new forms of worship. Folk masses and jazz services appeared, and guitars and film presentations were seen in worship. Although such innovation and experiment were only a novelty for many, the enthusiasm and popular styles of the music have had a continuing effect. In evangelical circles, it developed into the Contemporary Christian Music (CCM) industry.

In both churches and the American culture as a whole we are much more aware of the peoples and cultures of the world, and our appreciation for the music, ideas, and practices of other cultures has increased as well.

Language scholars have helped us recognize the ways the language we use shapes our beliefs and our actions, raising a call for more inclusive language for people and for God and for new images that reflect more contemporary life. Many new hymns and liturgies reflect our new awareness and provide fresh and relevant ways to sing and pray our faith. For the most part, the historical research and cultural and linguistic study have been broadly ecumenical and have led to a convergence of thinking about worship among Christians of many traditions.

As a result of the liturgical renewal movement, many denominations were introduced to the idea of an *ordo,* an overall pattern with deep historic roots that structures worship in Christian churches of widely differing theologies and histories. The *ordo* provides a flow to worship and includes the most basic actions of the Christian faith: gathering as an assembly in praise and prayer, sharing and interpreting the word of God, responding to the Word in sacraments of Holy Baptism and Eucharist, offering our gifts and lives in service, and going forth to live as

For the most part, the historical research and cultural and linguistic study have been broadly ecumenical and have led to a convergence of thinking about worship among Christians of many traditions.

We have found a great deal to celebrate in the results of the liturgical renewal movement so far.

Christ's disciples. Study of the early churches showed how they elaborated on this basic *ordo,* and many denominations came to adopt a common pattern that melded the ancient with later practices, translated and adapted for today's world. Church leaders in each denomination have worked to maintain those elements unique to their own traditions, while finding common ground in this overall pattern of worship and in the historic and theological importance of the sacraments of baptism and communion. This sifting process yielded the forms of worship that are found in hymnals and worship books now. The authors of this book have found a great deal to celebrate in the results of the liturgical renewal movement so far. Opportunities abound to enhance the meaning and depth of the weekly worship in our diverse congregations. At the same time, we are believers in the continuing process of worship reformation, "For God hath yet more light and truth to break forth from the Word."[2]

Our culture is changing in many ways. Many people have identified an emerging cultural era that has been labeled postmodern, and a flurry of books offer ways that churches should change to keep up. They call us to move away from the way the scientific worldview has shaped our Christian experience to be centered in the mind—and toward the inclusion of more of the heart. The church has lost its prominent place of influence in our culture, and the stories and assumptions of Christianity are no longer the foundation of our society. More and more of the people coming into our congregations will come without any previous experience of the church or from different denominational backgrounds. These and other fac-

---

*"Semper Reformanda,"* or "Always being reformed," was a rallying cry of our 16th-century forebears. A similar slogan, translated from Latin into English, is "The church reformed, always being reformed, according to Scripture."

tors will continue to influence our understanding of the patterns and meanings of worship.

## For Reflection and Discussion

1. What one or two things are most meaningful for you about worship in your congregation?
2. What makes them meaningful to you?

# Principles Guiding Worship

It is not our intention to promote a uniform order or service of worship. We value the diversity of individual congregational expression. We will not weigh one denominational pattern against another. We will first go beyond and behind these differences to identify and describe some principles that we think will be helpful as we reflect on our worship lives. With these principles in mind, we will walk through Sunday morning worship, raising questions and discussing the ways these principles offer opportunities for worship renewal and the ways we appropriate patterns to the service of Christ.

## I. Worship is the core of the church's life.

The act of worship makes us "church." All that we do beyond worship—teaching our children, serving the poor, gathering in small groups, maintaining buildings in which to meet—arises from our encounter with the living God in worship. Like Christians through the centuries, in worship we take part in the actions that form our identity as individuals and as Christians. We share the Word in reading and hearing Scripture and preaching; we welcome people into the community of Christ through baptism; we join together and are formed as the Body of Christ in Eucharist (the Lord's Supper); we offer ourselves and our resources

All that we do beyond worship—teaching our children, serving the poor, gathering in small groups, maintaining buildings in which to meet—arises from our encounter with the living God in worship.

*Worship stands at the center of congregational life (1) when there is an expectation of encounter with God in worship, (2) when preparation for worship is taken seriously by worship leaders and worshipers, (3) when the programmatic life of the congregation supports worship participation for people in all circumstances of life, and (4) when reflection on the worship is pervasive throughout congregational life.*

*Jane Rogers Vann, Gathered Before God*[3]

for God's work; and we are sent out with a vision of a world redeemed by God's love to serve all God's people.

This principle runs counter to those of some church-growth advocates. The "seeker service" movement, for example, suggests that participating in the full service of worship is a second or third step on the path to faith for those who are unchurched. Seeker churches remove symbols from sanctuaries, select shorter-than-usual passages of Scripture, and make use of pop-concert-quality music and staging to make the service more approachable. We believe that authentic, meaningful worship can also be approachable and inclusive and that such worship addresses the real needs of those who are seeking truth and meaning in life.

We recognize that not everyone comes into the church through worship. Some people come to know about the church through its community-service work or its outreach programs. They may become active in a church-based food pantry, breakfast program, or housing program, or a youth or young-adult group. This principle affirms, however, that wherever people enter the life of faith, they need the words of Scripture and the reflection upon those words as shared in the sermon; they need the prayers of the people and the acts of offering and dedication; they need the stories of Christ's life, death, and resurrection as lived out in Holy Communion; they need worship in a faith community to give it purpose. Worship is made complete by mission—by sending Christians to carry out the word, to embody Christ in the world. Even so, worship remains the spring from which the church's mission flows.

For Reflection and Discussion

1. What are the central purposes of the church?
2. If you have access to your church's mission statement, review it. Then identify differences, if any, from those you named in response to question 1. Could any of these purposes stand without the others?
3. How does worship fit these purposes? Is worship a purpose? A means to a goal? A goal in itself?
4. "The act of worship makes us church. All that we do beyond worship—teaching our children, serving the poor, gathering in small groups, maintaining buildings in which to meet—arises from our encounter with the living God in worship." Do you agree? Why or why not?
5. What would be the implications of making your congregation's worship life its top priority?
6. If worship already is the top priority, how do the rest of your congregation's activities reflect that?

2. Worship is the work of the people of God.

To many Protestants, liturgy is something done by "high-church" folk, like Catholics, Episcopalians, or Lutherans, but is not part of their own worship. We encourage all Christians to recover this term to

> [The Church] desires that all the faithful should be led to that full, conscious, and active participation in liturgical celebrations which is demanded by the very nature of the liturgy.
>
> *Constitution on the Sacred Liturgy*[4]

describe the structure and content of worship for one important reason: "Liturgy" means "the work of the people." Liturgy may have words written by one and may be led by a few, but it really exists only when it is enacted with the participation of all. So when we call our worship a liturgy, we are saying that worship involves the active participation of all the people.

How can this be? Certainly not everyone chooses hymns or writes the sermon. "Liturgy" in this case means that worship is shaped by and reflective of the individual and family, their lives and needs, and the ethnic and social cultures of the participants. It can also mean that worship is planned and led by more than one person. But even more, it means that those in the assembly have an important role in worship. Worship is not entertainment, nor is it "performed" by clergy or professional musicians for the people's benefit. It is, instead, *our* work (both clergy and laity), our words, our prayers, our songs. Our full and active participation in singing, listening, moving, praying, committing, and serving is crucial. When we open our hearts and minds in full participation, we enter into a relationship with the community of faith and into deeper relationships with God and with the world of which we are a part—relationships that transform us and increase the wholeness and meaning of our lives. If worship is to be truly transformative, then it asks for our utmost attention. For those who plan worship, the task is a sacred trust.

All of us need to prepare for worship, whether we are part of the assembled congregation or have a part

> It is our work, our words, our prayers, our songs. Our full and active participation in singing, listening, moving, praying, committing, and serving is crucial.

---

*Leitourgia* is a Greek word that comes from roots meaning "work" and "concerning the people or nation." In ancient Greece, before the time of Jesus, the word was used to refer to service done by citizens (of Athens, for example) on behalf of the community—the city or the country. While the word has taken on many other meanings since then (including several in the New Testament), liturgical scholars often cite this early meaning as a way of emphasizing that liturgy is something done by everyone.[5]

---

as a reader, preacher, presider, communion server, acolyte, choir member usher, or any other role. Whether the style is formal, with every word chosen in advance and every action prescribed, or more loosely crafted, with opportunities for spontaneous responses, worship is a time to be alert and open to the presence of the Spirit in our midst.

## For Reflection and Discussion

1. When you are not leading worship, how do you actively participate in worship?
2. Is there a particular time in worship when you feel truly engaged? If so, when?
3. Have you experienced times in worship when everyone was working together to worship God, when it seemed that everyone was engaged? If so, when has that happened?
4. Does your participation and that of others around you change your experience of God's presence in worship? If so, how?
5. What about your congregation's worship reflects its unique location and social and cultural makeup? What additional ways could the congregation's identity be reflected in worship?

## 3. Christianity is a communal faith.

Christians are formed in community and thrive as members of a community. This is one of the ways in which the Christian church can be countercultural, especially in Europe and North America. Our culture has become powerfully individualistic and self-indulgent. In many ways the churches were carried along into that rise of individuality in the culture and began placing greater importance upon personal experience than on the presence of Christ in the gathered assembly. From research into the early church and careful reading of Scripture, we have learned how

*How can we forget that our ability to pray we owe to the community and to tradition? We have learned how to pray by listening to the voice of prayer, having been a part of a community standing before God. Those who cherish genuine prayer, yet feel driven away from the houses of worship because of the sterility of public worship today, seem to believe that private prayer is the only way. Yet, the truth is that private prayer will not survive unless it is inspired by public prayer.*

Abraham Joshua Heschel, *Man's Quest for God*[6]

powerfully the community aspects of the first Christians affected the growth of the church. In a world of rigid hierarchy, the church of Christ was a community of equals, where all the baptized were valued as members of Christ's body. In the liturgical renewal movement, we are again recognizing how important the sacrament of baptism can be for establishing Christian identity.

We have the opportunity to recover that early principle of community in our worship. Christians are those who gather for praise and worship, to hear the word and to be united as one body in Christ through baptism and communion. This church is both holy and human. It is a fallible human institution, but it is also the people of God, blessed by the living Christ and able to trust in the presence of the Spirit when they are gathered and when they are scattered. This understanding of Christianity has important implications for our gathering to worship, and our covenants with one another within that gathered body. It affects our purpose in worship, the relationship of our personal devotional life to worship, the shape of our prayers during worship, and the meaning of the sacraments.

> Christians are those who gather for praise and worship, to hear the word and to be united as one body in Christ through baptism and communion.

For Reflection and Discussion

1. Recall a corporate worship event or a moment in worship when you felt God's presence. Was

the gathered worship community part of that experience? If so, how was the community important?

2. What draws you to worship each week?

3. How does worshiping with others help you relate to God? To other people?

## 4. Worship does not take us away from life but changes how we live.

Many of us who regularly attend church services have had occasion to wonder why we bother. Some worship seems out of touch with the real issues and concerns of life. When this separation from real life becomes a regular experience, however, something critical is missing from worship. We strongly believe that instead of leaving the world behind at the door the worshiping community should place the world alongside the Scriptures and the sacraments. When these are juxtaposed, we can see our lives and our world in a new way. From Scripture we learn that Christ came to redeem the whole world, not only individual sinners. In baptism we become part of the particular people of God, and in communion we renew our identity as Christ's body for the world. In worship we offer up our lives in all their complexity and interrelationships for transformation. Worship is meant to integrate faith and life.

> Worship is meant to integrate faith and life.

This principle has implications for all participants in worship. Clergy and worship leaders have a responsibility to listen to and address the true needs of the people. Worship should respond to the struggles and losses, the alienation and oppression, the smugness and blinders that affect the lives of people. The whole assembly should approach worship expecting that the words and actions of worship will be transformative of everyday life. We believe that the more of our lives we bring into our worship, and the more our faith spreads into all areas of our lives, then the more

> The more of our lives we bring into our worship, and the more our faith spreads into all areas of our lives, then the more vital our worship becomes.

vital our worship becomes. Worship becomes vitally important to life, even as it becomes more alive, filled with energy and passion.

When we say that worship does not take us away from life but changes how we live, we also mean that the events and issues of public life are appropriate topics for Scripture, prayer, and faithful reflection in worship. In the Scriptures we read of Jesus's active witness against the divisions of his society. He frequently spoke against the accumulation of wealth and misuse of power. When Christians gained the freedom to worship in the fourth century, the church took its worship out into the public square in the form of grand processions, highlighting worship itself as a witness in the world. When we see the world as the arena of Christ's continued work through the church, we shape people of faith and wholeness and announce that the realm of God is indeed near.

For Reflection and Discussion

1. What effect has worship had on how you live? Has it caused you to change your priorities? To respond differently to issues or people in your work, family, congregation, or the broader community? To spend time in different ways?
2. Have you experienced worship as a time of renewal and refreshment? If so, how important is this to you? Does it change the way you experience your daily life?

5. The patterns of worship shape how we pray and how we live.

Whatever our style of worship, it has a pattern—elements that are similar from week to week. Most often this pattern includes the order in which the elements of worship are arranged, but it also includes particular ways of speaking, forms of prayer, and ges-

*The deeper questions appear only when we allow worshipers to speak about how the liturgy has formed them in deep dispositions over time: in profound gratitude (receiving the world and other human beings as gifts), hope (even in the face of limits, suffering and death), or awe and delight (of the sense of grace in ordinary meals), because one has been present to many Eucharists—some dull, some alive.*

Don Saliers, *Worship as Theology: Foretaste of Glory Divine*[7]

tures such as bowed heads or raised hands. These patterns are worthy of our attention because they carry meaning, and they shape the way we understand our God, our relationships, and ourselves. How do we pray in our worship? Who prays? How is God addressed? Are the words individual or communal? Do we use "I" language or "we" language most often? Do we pray for the world or mostly for ourselves? Do we offer thanksgiving and praise or only entreaty or intercession?

When we learn to type or play the piano, we practice until our fingers know where the keys are and we no longer have to think about those details. When we worship, we are teaching our body how to move and our tongue how to speak or sing in ways that become ingrained in us, just as the location of keys becomes ingrained in a pianist. People who learn self-defense will practice responses to threats until those moves are second nature. We who worship a God of love should practice our moves so that love and service become second nature for us. When we develop habits of love and service in our worship and in our congregational relationships, we are more likely to embody them in our everyday lives. They become more than a Sunday habit. Practice of patterns of faithful acts is the basis for becoming and growing as Christian disciples. Our worship is the first and primary place where these habits and moves are learned, so we must attend to what our worship inscribes upon us; we must be sure that the words we sing and pray are words that will be good habits for life.

When we worship, we are teaching our body how to move and our tongue how to speak or sing in ways that become ingrained in us, just as the location of keys becomes ingrained in a pianist.

> Imagine a conversation with members of your congregation where, instead of asking, "What parts of worship should we expect children to sit through?" you ask, "With what worship practices do we want our youth and children to be familiar by the time they reach adolescence?"

As we walk through the acts of worship in the rest of this book, we will be speaking of some patterns that are worthy of being practiced and made part of our nature. We believe that these patterns can build good habits of Christian discipleship, as well as deepen the foundations of our faith, our knowledge of ourselves, and our relationships with others and with God.

For Reflection and Discussion

1. How do the patterns of worship affect you? What patterns are most helpful or meaningful? What patterns seem problematic for you, and why?
2. Are there elements of worship that you know by heart? Which ones? Do you remember them at times other than in worship?
3. In your personal prayer, do you find yourself repeating phrases or patterns from the prayers of worship? If so, which ones, and why?
4. Does the ritual of making an offering in worship affect how you respond to other needs and requests for support? If so, how?

## Worship on the Lord's Day

With these principles in mind, we can begin our discussion of Sunday worship. In a great many Protestant congregations, there are four movements of worship:

- Gathering
- Sharing the Word
- Responding in Thanksgiving
- Sending Forth

In the fourfold pattern of Protestant worship, the Scripture reading and sermon take place before the offering, the prayers of the people, and Holy Communion (when it is served). We are aware that a good number of congregations continue to use an order that places the sermon at the end of the worship service. This order was strongly influenced by camp meetings on the American frontier. The frontier services were occasional events intended to convert people to Christ rather than weekly gatherings of the faithful. The fiery sermon was usually followed by an altar call. Frontier-style services were highly memorable and moving, so people continued their pattern long after their original purpose had faded and most of those attending worship services were church members. In the discussion that follows, however, we will encourage use of the fourfold pattern described above, which has roots in the early church and allows the worshiping assembly to reflect on and assimilate the Word heard in Scripture and sermon as the assembly gives thanks and praise to God, prays for the world, and celebrates the feast at God's table. We believe that this worship order can serve those who are exploring faith as well as those whose faith is already well formed. Each movement is made up of smaller parts that we will call "elements" or "acts" of worship. Let us begin!

# Chapter 1

# Gathering

## *Preparation and Entering*

At the beginning of worship we open ourselves to the call of God's voice and attend to the movement of God's Spirit. We leave the isolation of our individual lives and gather with our community as the body of Christ. The elements of the worship service that begin with the prelude and end just before the Scripture reading within a typical Sunday service are together called the "gathering" or "entrance rites." These elements may include mutual greetings and hospitality, silent prayer or meditation, announcements, prelude or gathering songs, formal greeting, call to worship, invocation, prayer or act of confession and assurance, and passing of the peace.

Our goal in this book is not to provide a checklist for worship planners so that they can feel confident that they are doing worship "correctly." Neither is this list meant to suggest that every congregation

---

*To come into the presence of God is to stand on the mountain-top of God's compassion and justice and see the world from this vantage point. The journey is outward and inward—in both cases a widening of our everyday perspective. Outwardly, we enter into a wider circle of humanity. . . . But there is more—an inward "stretch" or widening of self. . . . One's unique history, gifts and eccentricities . . . and one's very ego are now rooted in something deeper than themselves—Christ.*

Robert Hurd, "A More Organic Opening"[1]

---

should be doing all these things every Sunday. Our purpose is to help you reflect on these elements and how they are or may be incorporated in the worship service of your congregation, in conversation with the principles expressed in our introduction.

Before we can reflect on how we approach and begin our worship service, however, we need to reflect on what it means to prepare for worship before the worship service begins. This preparation is twofold: each member of the Sunday morning congregation must prepare himself or herself for worship. Secondly, those with responsibility for planning and leading worship, including clergy and lay members who serve as worship planners or leaders, must give significant attention to the gathering as they plan for worship each week and during each liturgical season.

## Preparing Ourselves

Few of us give much thought to entering worship. On most Sundays, we consider ourselves fortunate to get out of bed, locate suitable clothing, swallow some coffee, and glance at the newspaper before scrambling out the door, driving to church, and sliding into the pew in time for the prelude. Add children, a partner, a spouse, or out-of-town guests to the mix, and the minimal goal of arriving in time for the first hymn may be the best one can do. At this pace, we might finally feel "centered" enough to "enter" worship toward the end of the sermon, or maybe not until the final hymn.

> On most Sundays, we consider ourselves fortunate to get out of bed, locate suitable clothing, swallow some coffee, and glance at the newspaper before scrambling out the door, driving to church, and sliding into the pew in time for the prelude.

*The Book of Worship of the United Church of Christ* (1986), describing what it means to prepare for and participate in worship, calls worship our offering to God. "This awareness places significant responsibility upon the people of God to live daily lives rooted and grounded in the gospel of Jesus Christ and to seek the presence of the Holy Spirit in prayer, study, planning, preparation, culminating in acts of worship filled with the grace and power of Pentecost."[2]

Imagine yourself as the pitcher for a baseball team who arrives just in time to throw the first pitch. Your muscles are cold and stiff. You haven't really honed in on the strike zone yet. Your mind is still on the traffic snarl you just faced, and not on the batter before you. Maybe by the second inning you are really ready to play, but by then the other team may have a good lead. Being prepared makes the difference.

We do deserve some credit: by gathering for worship weekly, we demonstrate that worship matters to us; we want the worship of God to be part of our lives. Yet it is difficult for worship to be a full and fulfilling part of our lives, let alone its life-giving core, if we do not allow adequate preparation time. We will not be able to listen for God's voice if we do not take time to make ourselves ready.

Preparing for worship entails three steps: *slowing down, making a transition,* and *warming up.* If we play an instrument, we set aside time before we perform for playing scales or other preparatory exercises. If we play a sport, dance, or practice yoga, we take time to warm up, elevate our heart rate, and stretch properly. These preparations help us make the most of our practice or performance because they help us move our focus from other parts of life to the activity at hand, so that we can engage in it more fully. Worship demands this same preparation.

*Slowing down* must start with the pace we establish on Sunday mornings before we arrive at church. It starts with the pace of our morning routine—the kind of music we listen to, the way we have breakfast, the tasks we try to accomplish. Rushing around on Sunday mornings and arriving barely in time will prevent us from making the transition, warming up, and entering worship well. All people who gather for worship need to prepare—not just the presiders, choir directors, or worship leaders. All of us can benefit from slowing our Sunday pace. Even when worship is lively and joyous, with upbeat music and a fast-paced

If we play an instrument, we set aside time before we perform for playing scales or other preparatory exercises. If we play a sport, dance, or practice yoga, we take time to warm up, elevate our heart rate, and stretch properly.

flow, we will still benefit by starting slowly and with calm and turning our focus toward the one whom we worship.

Our preparation for worship demands that we *make a transition:* we recognize that worship is not separate from our daily lives, that it is a special event within the patterns of life. We move from self-directed, outward-focused activity to a time of structured and active listening and openness to God's presence and guidance. As a special event, worship is *liminal:* it names and addresses the "limits" of our lives, where the edges of our ordinary lives meet the limitless reality of God. Like a child on a swing, we are most of the time in the safe middle, comfortably moving through daily pleasures and aggravations. But sometimes we are pushed to our limits. Then the swing is no longer safe or comfortable, and we experience birth, death, grief, or ecstatic joy.[3]

Because worship can name and address these limits, it can be a powerful experience. We may be moved to tears during worship as the hymns and prayers touch our sadness, loneliness, or anxiety. We may become angry during worship because the word from God we hear in Scripture touches us to the core and exposes the ways we have been harmed or wounded. We may be transported to a state of great joy, even ecstasy, during worship as we experience the good news of God's grace around the table in the company of our dear companions. In all of these situations, we have bumped into our limits and the power of these limits.

Since worship has the potential to affect us so powerfully, we need to pay adequate attention to our transition time. When we do not take this transition seriously, the power of the grief or anger or joy we experience in worship can be scary and overwhelming. By making transition, we are not trying to control or resist this power, but we are acknowledging that, by opening ourselves to God's word for us, we are accepting that worship may touch us deeply.

As a special event, worship is *liminal:* it names and addresses the "limits" of our lives, where the edges of our ordinary lives meet the limitless reality of God.

By making transition, we are acknowledging that worship may touch us deeply and that we are opening ourselves to God's word for us.

*Chronos* and *kairos* are both Greek words referring to kinds of time. *Chronos* is the ordinary, measured time in which we live: the passing of days and years, the human division of time into hours and minutes. *Kairos,* on the other hand, stands outside ordinary time. *Kairos* is the fullness of time, decisive time, or God's time. "The earliest portions of the New Testament are imbued with a sense of time as *kairos,*" says James White, "the right or proper time in which God has accomplished a new dimension of reality: 'The time [*kairos*] is fulfilled, and the kingdom of God has come near' (Mark 1:15)."[4]

If we have not experienced worship's power, perhaps we need to focus on opening ourselves to God's call in our transition time. How do we prepare to be touched so deeply? The simple acknowledgment that worship entails a transition from our daily routine (*chronos*) to a special pattern of being focused on God (*kairos*) begins the transition, but most of us need to do something more to bring it about. Perhaps on Saturday night or Sunday morning before worship we can take some time to reflect on our week. In a journal, in conversation, or in silent prayer, we bring to mind the hurts and pains, or the causes for celebration that we may bring to worship this week. By reflecting on our weekly experiences, we become more aware of what we need to let go of and offer to God. We become aware of how God might be calling us to something new, whether a relationship, a job, or a role. We become aware of what we need to celebrate, what we are thankful for, why we are offering God our praise.

In this transition we depart from the routine of our daily lives and enter a different pattern. The more attention we give to making this transition, the more natural it becomes. Our daily lives and our worship life are flowing into one another: we are bringing into our lives what we do on Sunday mornings, and what we do on Sunday mornings affects and drives what we do during the week. Moving from being alone or with a small circle of loved ones to being with our family of

Our daily lives and our worship life are flowing into one another: we are bringing into our lives what we do on Sunday mornings, and what we do on Sunday mornings affects and drives what we do during the week.

faith and greeting one another as we enter the church building completes our transition from every day to special day and begins our warm-up, getting us ready to worship.

Our *warm-up* begins when we approach and enter our common worship location. In some congregations people greet one another before the worship service in a narthex or other room where there may be refreshments provided over which people can meet and reconnect. Some of us attend a Christian education class or a music rehearsal before worship. All of us are worship participants, and we all need to warm up.

At the appropriate time, we make our way to the sanctuary. We get the things we will need for worship: a printed order of worship, perhaps a hymnal or a songbook. Children may select some crayons and a children's worship bulletin. Perhaps the basket to collect food for the food pantry is in the sanctuary, and of course we have our donation for the offering. We make sure that these are in an accessible place so that we can share them when that moment in worship arrives. In some congregations, we remember our baptism by marking ourselves with water from the baptismal font placed just inside the sanctuary where all will pass. The opening of worship, whether it is an instrumental prelude, a time of silence, or a time of chanting or singing, gives us time to complete our warm-up and ready ourselves to participate fully.

We have slowed down, made transition, and warmed up. We have greeted one another in the name of Christ and have prepared our hearts and minds for worship.

## Planning for Gathering

In each congregation, one or more people have responsibility for planning the Sunday morning worship service. Clergy will certainly be involved in this

A worship-planning committee can be created to deal with one liturgical season, or a standing committee can help plan worship for each liturgical season in turn. Also, a planning committee may have several subgroups that draw upon or nurture the skills and gifts of the wider congregation in such areas as visual arts, Scripture reading, drama, and dance. Crucifers and acolytes and even choir members can improve their skills to energize a procession by doing more than just walking in a line. Many people discover that they develop latent gifts for worship planning, art, drama, and Scripture reading through participation in such a planning group. How might such groups enrich the ways your congregation gathers?

task, but we hope that others are involved as well: musicians, readers, dramatists, or a worship-planning committee.

Our entrance and gathering rites deserve special attention. How we gather and enter worship will set the tone for the rest of the service. A somber and rigid gathering sets a certain tone. A gathering that is a chaotic afterthought sets another tone. Those who are involved in planning worship need to attend to what seem like minor details, and many people need training and rehearsal. Are the ushers ready to help with hearing-assistance devices, large-print bulletins, and handicap-accessible seating? Are there enough ushers and greeters on hand to answer the questions of visitors or newcomers? ("Where is the nursery?" "Where is an accessible restroom?") Are acolytes, choir members, crucifers (cross-bearers), readers, and presiders prepared for the processional? How will the congregants know that they are invited to take part in the processional or the responsive reading? These and other details in our gathering and entering demand thought and attention as we prepare for worship.

For Reflection and Discussion

1. What part of worship would you most miss if it were not included? Why?

2. How well does the gathering portion of worship in your congregation draw the community together? Why?

3. What can we learn from this to make our congregation's Gathering more successful?

4. How do you prepare to come to worship?

5. Are you ready when the opening words are said or sung? If so, what do you do that makes you ready ? If not, when do you feel like you are worshiping?

6. How do you respond to the suggestions above for personal preparation? Do you think such conscious effort would make a difference in your experience of worship? Why or why not? How might you better prepare yourself to join with the community in worship?

7. What could we do as a congregation to help people prepare to fully participate in worship?

## Entrance Rites

Now that we have thought about preparation, we can reflect on the elements of our gathering or entrance rites, asking how our congregation's way of enacting these rites might reflect our principles.

---

Hospitality is one of the foundations of Christian faith. If we are truly to gather as the people of God, we must learn to welcome one another with warmth and care. Congregations that see welcome as a primary mission not only attract and hold more members, but they also share a greater commitment to one another and greater vitality in all aspects of their communal life. Two good resources for both the theology and the practice of hospitality are Lucien Richard, O.M.I., *Living the Hospitality of God* (Mahwah, N.J.: Paulist Press, 2000), and Elizabeth Rankin Geitz, *Entertaining Angels : Hospitality Programs for the Caring Church* (Harrisburg, Pa.: Morehouse, 1993).

*The convergence at the entryway of the building that bears our name—church—isn't quite like any other. Baptism, not blood or a common interest in sports or theater, has brought us here. Once we are here, we make no distinctions among persons. What binds us is stronger than age, sex, education, politics, wealth, common interests. Here there is no stranger, no first and no last.*
Gabe Huck, *Sunday Mass Five Years from Now*[5]

## Mutual Greeting and Hospitality

Both the casual meeting of friends and acquaintances arriving together or sharing a cup of coffee or tea before worship and the more organized tasks of a hospitality team that welcomes newcomers are part of the greeting. These greetings are an important part of melding scattered individuals into one body for worship. Ideally, this greeting takes place in a narthex or fellowship area rather than in the worship space itself, for two reasons. On one hand, it allows people who want a time of silence or prayer before worship to sit in the quiet sanctuary without distraction. The second reason is more symbolic. Although it is rare that the whole assembly enters the worship space in procession together, the physical action of moving into a different place signals a change, the final transition to worship. There was a time when people in many church traditions felt that a sanctuary was a holy place and that the playing of an organ prelude was the sign for silence and reverence. As we have become more casual and more practical (perhaps the term is cynical), the prelude remains a sign to enter the worship space, but conversations and greetings usually continue. Entering the worship space as if we were finding seats at a ball game diminishes the symbolic value of entering the space where we will worship God together. We hope that communities can recover the sense of sacred space to the extent that they can honor the special qualities of events about to take place.

Congregations with one primary public entrance to the worship space and a greeting space outside it are also able to concentrate their hospitality team. When people enter from several doors, good hospitality suggests an usher or greeter at each entrance so that everyone is welcomed to worship, even the most stalwart and active volunteers.

## Entrance or Gathering Music

In many congregations an organ or piano prelude provides the opening music, often in a meditative style. If this is the practice that your congregation chooses, or chooses for a liturgical season, it is appropriate to work at making the worship space a quiet haven, so that those who want to listen or meditate can do so. In other congregations, the opening of worship is more like a party or fiesta getting underway. In this case, your worship planning team will want to consider music and sanctuary activities that invite people to enter and join in.

Your congregation may want to consider music during the gathering that is participatory. Singing demands people's attention, and the words begin to focus minds on what is about to happen. Simple chants or repetitive songs of praise can be a wonderful invi-

*Your congregation may want to consider music during the gathering that is participatory.*

Contemporary Christian "praise" choruses are perhaps the most well known examples of music used during the gathering moments of worship. However, songs that focus exclusively on praise and celebration may not be appropriate for seasons or services that are more reflective or penitential. Also, many mainline Protestant congregations struggle to find contemporary choruses that are theologically appropriate for their congregations.[6] The simple chants of the ecumenical Taizé Community in France and the Iona Community of Scotland (both available through GIA Publications, Chicago) can be a good place to start. They are simple and engaging and include a variety of moods and themes. You may also find helpful resources at www.tributariesoffaith .org, which gathers links to progressive mainline musicians who are also writing music for the church.

tation to people to enter the worship space and begin worship. This type of sung meditation can help people make the transition into worship by calming and centering them. At the same time, sung meditation serves to gather us into community by joining our individual voices together in one body of Christ.

Whether organ prelude or opening songs, this music signals that it is time to turn our attention to worship. Casual greeting time has passed. Respect for one another and our preparation for worship means we should be present and ready when the prelude begins. Some of us fight a chronic struggle to be on time, and there will always be latecomers; but as worship planners, we have a responsibility to the majority to begin on time and not extend the preliminaries in the hope of getting everyone into the sanctuary before the call to worship. The prelude or other opening music should be planned as the beginning of worship. It is neither an opportunity for the organist to show off nor a time when just anything will do. It serves to warm people up for worship, and it deserves care and attention and full integration into our worship planning for theme and mood and season.

## Silent Prayer or Meditation

Some people need a time of silent prayer or meditation to help them focus and become ready for worship. Ideally, people should be able to meditate in the worship space itself. However, in some congregations no wall or partition separates the narthex or gathering area from the sanctuary, so the worship space is not quiet during the greeting and gathering time. In some settings, choirs are rehearsing in the sanctuary, and leaders and presiders are doing last-minute preparation. Although we recognize that multiple services or limited space can create great difficulties for reducing the last-minute rush, we would encourage congregations to look for ways to minimize the buzz, not only to allow for meditation in the worship space without undue distraction but also to enhance the sense of entrance and to begin worship with calm and order. A space that is quiet or has gentle music playing can encourage early arrivals to enter and center themselves. Each congregation will have to balance the advantage of quietness in the sanctuary against the encounters of the greeting time, and the type of mood or activity that seems appropriate to the congregation and liturgical season. It may be that a chapel or other space will better serve those desiring meditation time before worship.

## First Words

What are the first words heard in your service? Are they formal or casual? In some congregations, the service opens with a formal greeting or call to worship. In many, it is, "Good Morning!" and people often respond with the same words. This has become an opening litany, part of the liturgy, even if not really on the worship plan. Formalists among us urge us to exchange this common and worldly greeting for one more biblical and specific to our Christian faith. Others feel that "Good morning!" is a perfectly appropriate adoption from the broader culture because what God has created is good, and we wish to share that good with everyone.

Listen carefully to what is said in your congregation. Who is welcomed—everyone or only visitors? Is there a distinction between "we," the members and staff, and "you," the visitor?

Whether formal or casual, many congregations follow the greeting with a statement of welcome. Listen carefully to what is said in your congregation. Who is welcomed—everyone or only visitors? Is there a distinction between "we," the members and staff, and "you," the visitor? According to a recent study, hospitality and welcome are key emphases in a vital and caring congregation. The opening statement is a key expression of the congregation's welcome.

## Announcements

It is a rare congregation that chooses to eliminate spoken announcements from worship, although many recognize that announcements can get a service off to a slow or even discordant start. For those announcements that must be spoken during Sunday morning worship, the very beginning of the service or the very end of the service is probably the best time to make them. Many congregations include announcements at some point in the middle of the service because if they were placed at the beginning, no one would be there to hear them! If announcements are to be made at the beginning of worship, the congregation will need to get used to arriving on time. If they are placed at the end of worship, they can be tied naturally to our being sent forth, will be heard even by latecomers, and are more likely to be brief.

Most congregations use a printed bulletin that includes announcements. Some print church news and events on a separate sheet or insert that can be taken home and posted. When information is printed in ways that are easy to read and refer to, only the most important or urgent need be repeated aloud. Congregations that use projection screens often prepare announcement slides that run as people gather and are seated. Being sure that everything is ready in time to be printed or projected is part of being prepared for

---

Marcia McFee has written a litany to incorporate announcements, joys, and concerns as part of the Gathering Movement of worship.

*Announcements:*
L: We thank God for these opportunities for fellowship and service.
P: Thanks be to God!
*Joys:*
L: We give thanks to God for these blessings.
P: Thanks be to God!
*Concerns:*
L: For all these people and all who are in need,
P: Hold your people near, O God!
L: Let us take a moment to center our hearts on God.
The litany is followed by a meditative musical interlude of about two minutes.[7]

---

worship. In some settings the announcements could be made in the narthex or fellowship area if that is where nearly all people are gathering and an adequate sound system allows all to hear.

Even though we often wish to minimize announcements, they serve two important and related functions. First, they remind us of the work we do together as the people of God and so help us gather into one body. Second, they connect what happens in the rest of the week to what happens in worship. Consider discarding the term "announcements" and saying "church events" or "our shared life and service" or some other descriptive term. The way we label and introduce and manage announcements can make them a welcome addition to worship rather than an interruption.

Some congregations add a time of sharing joys and concerns to the gathering rite. People offer brief statements about personal or public concerns to be part of the congregation's worship. These may be incorporated into prayers later in the service.

## Call to Worship

The call to worship is precisely that: the call or summons to the whole community of God's people gathered in a congregation to join in the praise and worship of God. In most cases, the entire community should participate in it. Usually this works best as some kind of brief, responsive exchange between a designated leader and the assembly. The assembly's part may be as brief as an "Amen" or "And also with you." The following apostolic greeting calls attention to the focus of worship:

> *Leader:* The grace of our Lord Jesus Christ, the love of God and the communion of the Holy Spirit be with you.
> *People:* And also with you.

*Repetition and rhythm in the liturgy are to be fostered. No rule is more frequently violated by the highly educated and well meaning, who seem to think that never having to repeat anything is a mark of effective communication. Yet rhythm, which organizes repetition, makes things memorable, as in music, poetry, rhetoric, architecture, and the plastic arts no less than in liturgical worship.*

Aidan Kavanagh, *Elements of Rite: A Handbook of Liturgical Style.*[8]

Many congregations use a greeting like this as the whole of the call to worship. Others use a greeting as the opening words followed by a longer litany that introduces the theme or topic for the worship or relates to the season of the church year and invites the gathered assembly into the time and space of worship. When the words in a call to worship stay consistent and brief over a period of time such as a liturgical season or a whole year, people who do not read well, including children, the visually impaired, and the developmentally disabled, can learn them and participate in them. Even the most literate benefit from having certain words inscribed upon their hearts. For a call to worship that is repeated weekly and memorized, four brief lines (two for the leader, two for the assembly) work well. The words still need to be printed or projected on a screen, no matter how often used, so that newcomers are equally included.

Even the most literate benefit from having certain words inscribed upon their hearts.

Scripture is the most appropriate source for the call to worship, whether as a direct quote or adapted for the situation. Many books are available to pastors and worship planners that refer to one or all of the weekly lectionary readings in a call to worship. The goal of this type of call to worship is to preview the Scripture readings and give worship a consistent scriptural thread. This approach assumes a greater familiarity with Scripture than many people have.

Calls to worship can also be sung by the whole congregation and may be part of the gathering music.

Whether the call to worship is short or longer, sung or spoken, repeated or varied each week, using a variety of images and Scriptures will enrich the congregation's worship experience.

## Choral Introit

In some congregations, a choral introit (from Latin roots meaning "entrance" or "to go in") serves as the call to worship. In other congregations, a choral introit may be a sung response to the call to worship. Because we believe that participation is a key principle, we would suggest that the words be printed in the bulletin or projected so that all can understand. A sung exchange, led by a cantor or choir member, allows the whole assembly to participate. Again, repeating the same exchange over the course of a given liturgical season will help people to learn it and to participate actively.

## Hymns and Songs

There have been jokes among preachers that refer to everything other than a sermon in the service as three hymns and a prayer. Humor always has some basis in truth, and in many congregations those three hymns are beginning, middle, and end, without much thought as to how they function in the pattern of worship. Other congregations use hymns and sung responses more and make sure that each suits its place and the theme.

---

Gabe Huck reminds us that the opening of worship "must not be about ministers and musicians taking possession of the liturgy."[9] That is, the opening words, music, or procession should draw everyone into participation from the beginning instead of creating a model of active leaders and passive watchers. In what ways do the gathering rites of your congregation ensure that worship is engaging everyone?

---

In some congregations, an entrance or opening hymn immediately follows the prelude. In others, the first song may follow the call to worship. Some use both. Either may include a procession. A hymn selected for the opening of worship works well when it is easy to sing and well known. Because praise is an important aspect of the Gathering, the hymn should ideally praise God the Creator or Jesus Christ, or it may invoke the presence of the Holy Spirit in the worship gathering. Some hymns and songs do all of these and call people to worship as well.

Since almost anything can be set to music, nearly any element of worship may be sung. We encourage congregational singing in whatever style suits your worship. Singing together has lost favor in many secular circles, and some who come into the church may find singing a bit uncomfortable at first, but the church has a long and rich tradition of hymns and songs that draw people together and reach into hearts to teach the faith in ways that the spoken word is unable to do.

## Processions

Processions typically take place during a hymn. The processional hymn should be well known, easy to sing, and have a good pace for walking. Even experienced choir members have trouble walking to unfamiliar music. Processions can be simply two acolytes bearing candles and the pastor. Many include the choir. They may include a cross-bearer, someone carrying the Bible, a thurifer (who carries the incense vessel), banner carriers, additional clergy, dancers, and lay readers. Processions are meant to serve as a festive and celebratory entry into worship, and it is wonderful when the whole congregation participates and enters into worship together. Realistically, your church building's architectural design may not include a narthex or other space large enough for the

You might want to experiment with a community-wide procession for important times such as Palm Sunday or Pentecost.

*Some years ago, I spent an afternoon caught up in a piece of sewing I was do-ing. The wastebasket near my sewing machine was filled with scraps of fabric cut away from my project. This basket of discards was a fascination to my daughter, Annika, who, at the time, was three years old. . . . When it had been silent too long, I tracked her whereabouts to the back garden. . . . She was fix-ing the scraps to the top of a pole with great sticky wads of tape. . . . I asked her what she was doing. Without taking her eyes from her work she said, "I'm making a banner for a precession [sic]. I need a precession so that God will come and dance with us." With that, she solemnly lifted her banner to flutter in the wind and got up to dance.*

Gertrude Mueller Nelson, "Christian Formation of Children: The Role of Ritual and Celebration."[10]

Of course we know that God is already present, but this is the moment to ac-knowledge God's presence and to express our hope for God's action within the worship on this day.

congregation to gather, and such a procession might be hard to organize every week. However, you might want to experiment with a community-wide proces-sion for important times such as Palm Sunday or Pen-tecost. If you undertake such a procession, remember that planning, accommodation for the physically chal-lenged, and communication will be important, so that all people can participate and see all that happens. Key leaders will need to rehearse the route of the pro-cession, and ensure that the route is clearly designated for people to follow.

### Prayer of the Day

A brief prayer is a very common element in the Gath-ering movement. It is a time to welcome God into our

A *collect* always has the same basic form: (1) an address to God; (2) a refer-ence to some characteristic or act of God as a ground for prayer; (3) a brief, direct prayer of petition; (4) a concluding doxology, offering the prayer to the triune God. Collects are usually specific to the Scripture texts, liturgical season, or theme of the day. The most well known selection of *collects* within Protestantism may be those written by Thomas Cranmer (1489-1556), found in the *Book of Common Prayer* of the Episcopal Church. For a well-written variety of more contemporary collects, see *A New Zealand Prayer Book*.[11]

Many Protestant traditions, prayer books, or worship books contain a good variety of collects. Collects require discipline to write because of their formal structure and the challenge to keep them very brief. If your congregation chooses to use a collect regularly, a group of writers in your congregation may want to experiment with writing collects using the traditional structure.

worship. Of course we know that God is already present, but this is the moment to acknowledge God's presence and to express our hope for God's action within the worship on this day. The prayer focuses us and centers us on the God whom we gather to praise.

The prayer may be highly structured or quite freeform. One type of prayer of the day is a collect, a very ancient and structured form of prayer in the Western church. It is usually a formal prayer that is trinitarian in structure (see sidebar).

A prayer of invocation does not have the same ancient tradition or structure as a collect, but it is quite common in some denominations today. A prayer of invocation may be less structured or even extemporaneous, but like collects, prayers of invocation are brief, celebrate God's acts, and call upon the Trinity to open us to God's presence without moving away from the focus on praise. The pastor or liturgist may offer the prayer of invocation, or it can be said in unison or as a litany.

## Prayer of Confession and Words of Assurance

The Hebrews offered confession to God in the form of Psalms (see Psalm 51). Therefore, confession is an ancient practice within our Judeo-Christian tradition. Confession is a type of prayer in which we acknowledge our sin and the abuse of our God-given free will. We acknowledge this sin before God and before each other, and we recognize that our sin keeps us from being the people God has created us to be. At the same time, because God's grace has been made known to us in Jesus Christ, we know that our sin is never the final word. God always has the final word, and this word is forgiveness and grace. Therefore any prayer of confession ends with words of assurance or absolution, which proclaim God's love, acceptance, and forgiveness.

Confession and assurance or absolution can be placed at any of several points in in worship. At times in church history human sin and penitence were the prominent focus of worship. This emphasis has changed in most churches, but traces remain in services that begin with confession before moving to praise, as some Lutheran services do. Other traditions see confession as a natural result of our praise. God's goodness and love inspire us to see our shortcomings and to confess them, seeking reconciliation with God and one another before proceeding with the Service of the Word. Presbyterian resources suggest this order, for example. The *United Methodist Hymnal* places the acts of confession and reconciliation, including the passing of the peace, immediately before the eucharistic prayer when communion is celebrated.

The Protestant Reformers put an emphasis on general confessions in the assembly. Recent worship reforms have sought to soften the often harsh quality of these historic prayers of confession. Corporate prayers of confession are among the most difficult prayers to write. Prayers of confession must never condemn us to the exclusion of God's grace. Indeed, it is in light of God's grace that we find the will and the courage to express our confession. The prayer should address our shortcomings without being so specific that we feel singled out for shame or are able to tell ourselves that it doesn't apply to us. Prayers of confession should never single out certain groups of people or specific acts. We are all human, so we are all separated from God and therefore are prone to sin, and yet God's grace is for all of us. Therefore our prayers of confession must be general and include all

God's goodness and love inspire us to see our shortcomings and to confess them, seeking reconciliation with God and one another before proceeding with the Service of the Word.

people—laity and clergy. Prayers of confession should not be so brief that they trivialize sin or minimize the harm and wounds we inflict on one another. But neither should prayers of confession be so long that God's grace, proclaimed in the words of assurance, seems minor in comparison. One way to do this is to confess together the sin of our society and to leave space for silent personal confession before announcing God's grace. For example, the prayer may confess that our society's emphasis on getting rich quick feeds the popularity of gambling, especially among those who can least afford to lose. Individuals may recognize themselves in the general prayer and confess their own gambling in their silent prayers.

The words of assurance and absolution remind us of God's grace and forgiveness. In the sacramental tradition of the Roman Catholic Church, only priests can provide absolution and proclaim God's forgiveness in the name of Jesus Christ. Among Protestants, it is usually the clergy who speak the words of assurance to the rest of the assembly. Although it is the role of worship leaders, both clergy and lay, to be Christ's representatives to the assembly, we know they are also humans in need of God's grace. It is becoming a tradition in some congregations for the leader to proclaim, "In the name of Jesus Christ, you are forgiven," and for the congregation to repeat back, "In the name of Jesus Christ, you are forgiven." Also, we might want to reflect on what happens when it is only the clergy who proclaim God's forgiveness week in and week out. This clergy-centered pattern opens the possibility that we see clergy as the possessors or mediators of God's mercy, when in fact this mercy belongs to God alone. When only ordained clergy speak the words of assurance, it can appear that the rest of the assembly (but not the presider) is in need of mercy or assurance. Your congregation might want to consider varying the person who leads the prayer of confession and proclaims the words of assurance.

We might want to reflect on what happens when it is only the clergy who proclaim God's forgiveness week in and week out.

## Other Acts of Praise

We respond to the proclamation of God's mercy and assurance with words of praise and thanksgiving. In many Protestant liturgies, the congregation sings the words of either the ancient "Gloria Patri," or the "Gloria in Excelsis." Both of these are doxologies, songs of praise. The traditional text of the Gloria Patri most commonly sung in Reformed and Methodist Churches is: "Glory be to the Father, and to the Son, and to the Holy Ghost; as it was in the beginning, is now, and ever shall be, world without end. Amen." Lutherans and Anglicans may use the Gloria in Excelsis. One variation of the beginning of the Gloria in Excelsis is, "Glory to God in the highest and peace to God's people on earth."

Most of our Protestant worship books or hymnals provide versions of the "Gloria Patri" that use gender-inclusive, or gender-neutral trinitarian imagery, replacing "Father" with "Creator" or "Source" and "Son" with "Christ." Some of our worship books and hymnals also provide us with lovely variations of both the "Gloria Patri" and the "Gloria in Excelsis," some of which come from ecumenical communities such as Taizé or Iona. Other variations on the "Gloria" reflect the multicultural diversity of the people of God. Argentine musician Pablo Sosa's "Gloria" and the South African "Masithi" are both included in *The New Century Hymnal*'s service music. Whichever option your congregation might choose, it is good to bear in mind the advice given above: make a selection and stick to it over a liturgical season or series of seasons so that those who do not read words or music may more easily offer their praise to God.

It is not necessary or altogether historical to respond to the words of assurance with either of these traditional doxologies, although most reformed Protestant orders of worship have included one or the

The Good News of God's love and mercy despite our errors and waywardness deserves our sung or spoken words of praise, whether in one of these historic doxologies, the words of a psalm, or another song or hymn of praise.

other at some point during the entrance rites. But the good news of God's love and mercy despite our errors and waywardness deserves our sung or spoken words of praise, whether in these historic doxologies, the words of a psalm, or another song or hymn of praise.

## Passing of the Peace

The passing of the peace of Christ is another variable or movable element of our entrance rites. It sometimes serves as a greeting and comes right after a call to worship. It is also an act of reconciliation, and in many churches it follows the confession and assurance, before or after or sometimes instead of a Gloria. Reconciliation is also appropriate before the communion liturgy, and the peace is placed there in some traditions. In many congregations, this formal exchange of peace is absent altogether, having been absorbed into the more informal acts of greeting that take place before the worship service; or people may be asked to greet one another during the gathering or elsewhere in the service. These other greetings can acknowledge the centrality of hospitality in Christian life, but sometimes become a chatty distraction from the worship setting.

The passing of the peace originates in the "kiss of peace" described in the letters of the apostle Paul, and so is grounded in the earliest days of our tradition. In many congregations, the peace is still symbolized with a kiss, hug, handshake, or other exchange of touch.

---

How might your congregation include people who have difficulty with the passing of the peace? Could they bow to others as they say, "The peace of Christ"? We know of one congregation where the friends of a survivor of abuse regularly "run interference" by shielding her from well-meaning people who do not know or understand her history. This assistance enables her to participate in her own way and to work toward healing.

---

Because this is a person-to-person greeting and blessing and reflects the incarnation of God into human life, it is fitting that our exchanges of peace include the kind of physical action that other greetings do. Touching one another reinforces the meaning of the words: the laying on of hands is a basic sacramental gesture of blessing for us as Christians.

We also need to be sensitive to the way that touch is trivialized and sexualized in Western and American cultures as well as to the different traditions surrounding touch among peoples of non-Western cultures. Further, we need to be sensitive to those who have been harmed by touch that was unwanted and unwarranted. A hug or a kiss should never be forced upon any member of an assembly. That being said, a gentle handshake, with a sincere and sympathetic utterance of peace, may pave the way for those who have been harmed by touch to begin to receive touch that is appropriate and loving within the midst of the Christian assembly.

The passing of the peace can be a moment when we acknowledge to one another that we have heard and proclaimed God's forgiveness and our forgiveness of one another. Our passing of the peace cannot be an act of cheap grace or a substitute for the ongoing work of healing or reconciliation among people between whom true harm has passed. When we pass the peace of Christ within the context of Christian worship, particularly with those with whom we have had serious disagreement, these moments can be times of transformation when anger or bitterness is eased, and we recognize our common humanity. The passing of the peace within the Christian assembly may begin a deeper process of reconciliation between people, or it may mark the culmination of such a process. However, no one should be forced or expected to enter into a gesture or exchange of peace with someone who has done her or him serious harm before feeling ready to exchange such gestures or words.

Gathering rites (1) help us make a transition from daily life to worship mode, (2) unite the assembly as one body, (3) open us to God's presence, and (4) ready us to hear God's word. Which of these does your congregation do well? In which areas might you explore new possibilities?

It is helpful to newcomers and regular participants in any worshiping community to know what to expect, and this awareness is especially important during the passing of the peace. The peace should be a ritual that includes words and gesture: a firm handshake, a deliberate "The peace of Christ be with you," and a reply, "And also with you." It might be helpful to describe the ritual in the worship bulletin. Or the presider may invite people to "share the peace of Christ by shaking hands, proclaiming God's peace, and responding 'and also with you.'"

We have reflected on what it means to prepare for worship, to gather with the community of God's people in a particular congregation, and to enter worship. Now we turn our attention to the proclamation of God's Word for us in the Sunday morning assembly.

For Reflection and Discussion

1. What entrance rites does your congregation regularly use? (Refer to your worship bulletins to refresh your memory.)
2. How does each element relate to those before and after it? How does meaning or energy flow from element one to another?
3. How does each serve to welcome and gather people as one body to worship and ready them to hear the Word read and proclaimed?
4. Are there elements described in the book or that you know from other traditions that would be beneficial additions to your Gathering rites? If so, which ones, and why do you think they would be beneficial?

# Chapter 2

# The Service of the Word
## *Sharing Together in the Word of God*

Everyone loves a good story. Throughout our lives we share stories with each other: family stories, sports stories, life stories, funny stories, and sad stories. In our worship we come together to tell and hear the stories of our faith, both historic and personal. We have prepared ourselves for worship and have gathered as the family of God, and now we settle in to hear God's word for us today. Much like a family gathered at the home place for a holiday meal, the church, the body of Christ, gathers to hear and to tell its own family stories. The church prepares to hear of God's working in the past and to join in that story as the stories become its own.

Rather than merely sitting back and listening, the congregation brings its own story as a community and the stories of each of its members as part of the whole Christian story. The gathered people listen to God's word for them today as they hear the stories of God's people from the past. As the story of the Exodus is read, the listeners are drawn in to follow the pillar of fire through the uncertain wilderness. As the crowd of people outside Jerusalem wave palms and shout "Hosanna," the crowd of today shouts along with them. As the New Testament writer bids the listener to "walk in the light," the followers of today walk as well. This listening is not passive but active. It is participatory—a doing, an action. The words we

*When your parishioners gather on a Sunday morning, they each bring their unique immediate and distant pasts. And God, who faithfully works with us, whispers a unique word to each one . . . How God works with your sermon with faithful Old Mrs. Brown may be quite different from how God works with your sermon with the new young man in town who just happened to drop in to today's service. . . . Therefore, the sermon, even though it is presented in its own integrity as a single whole, is in reality a multiple event. One preaches as many sermons as there are persons in the congregation.*
Marjorie Hewitt Suchocki, *The Whispered Word: A Theology of Preaching*[1]

hear and the songs we sing are not just entertaining words; they carry a word from God, and each one of us can be engaged in discernment of that word.

We believe that we gather as the church to *do* worship—not merely to observe what is happening up front. We are all participants in the celebration. In other words, our attendance at worship is more like going to a meeting of a storytellers' group than it is like going to a movie or a lecture.

Gathering to read and hear Scripture is an ancient activity for the people of God. When the children of Sarah and Abraham were given the great commandment to "love the Lord your God with all your heart, and with all your soul, and with all your might," they were exhorted to "keep these words, recite them to your children and talk about them" (Deut. 6:5–9). From the day of resurrection, followers of the risen One gathered to share their stories of new life. Eventually, these stories were written down and passed among various communities and were collected into what we call the Bible—the Scriptures of our faith.

The congregation gathers as one body to hear and respond to the word read and proclaimed. Our baptism marks us as the people of God and calls us to attend to the stories of Scripture as our stories—the difficult, perhaps strange, stories as well as the ones that are familiar and easy to understand. In our listening, we hear God's grace for us as individuals as well as for the life of the church and the world. The Holy Spirit moves in and among all of us—in the members of the congregation as well as the preacher.

As we have said, worship has patterns; similar elements are therefore present from week to week. Readings and responses that occur in a repeated order build familiarity in the community: worship is not completely reinvented each week. This familiarity allows worshipers to feel a sense of ownership; it enhances their listening because they know what to expect and can be ready to hear the word of God. Yet, within the order there is variety—the readings, psalms, hymns, and sermon all change each week. The order suggested here is seen in many contemporary worship resources. While the styles of worship may vary within and among traditions, the general shape remains the same.

The service of the word may include some or all of the following:

Prayer for Illumination
First Reading
Psalm
Second Reading
Song or Anthem
Gospel Reading
Sermon/Proclamation
Response

In his book *Liberating Rites,* Tom Driver speaks of the human need for both rituals of stability and rituals of liberation. We *need* some things to be the same each week—especially when our lives are chaotic. We also need rituals that are liberating, that help to break us out of old patterns that hold us back from becoming more like Christ.[2] How might attention to both of these kinds of needs—stability and liberation, tradition and creativity, serenity and flux—be built into your worship-planning process?

# Preparing Ourselves and Planning for the Service

We have talked about preparation for worship—getting to church, preparing ourselves, our families, our church for gathering to worship. But how can we prepare to listen to the word of God? Throughout the week, members of the faith community can prepare as individuals and families. One way to prepare is through a period of daily personal worship. This worship might include the offering of prayers, a time of silent listening, and readings from Scripture. Congregations may encourage personal worship by printing in a parish newsletter or weekly bulletin the Scripture passages that will be read in the future weeks of worship. Families may want to use them to worship together. Church school curricula may provide family devotional resources that will connect with weekly worship. Weekly Bible study groups that anticipate the Sunday lessons also prepare people to listen and participate. Such preparation alerts our senses, hearts, and minds to the working of God's Spirit in our lives and in the world around us. Then, when we gather as the body of Christ, we are ready to hear together the word of God for us today.

Again, taking time to plan the service well in advance is also important. Preachers sometimes excuse Saturday-night sermon writing by explaining that they are waiting for the Holy Spirit. As preachers and worship planners, we have found that the Holy Spirit is always at work and that wonderful worship can be planned weeks ahead and still be timely and relevant. The Holy Spirit knows better than we do what might be needed, and when we prepare with open hearts, the Spirit works through us. Not being prepared can mean that we don't leave time to be open to God's presence and that opportunities are lost. Planning further in advance, on the other hand, gives ideas and

---

*Such preparation alerts our senses, hearts, and minds to the working of God's Spirit in our lives and in the world around us. Then, when we gather as the body of Christ, we are ready to hear together the word of God for us today.*

*Planning further in advance gives ideas and scriptural themes time to marinate, soaking up the flavor of the world around us.*

In some congregations, lay members have a much larger role than others. They may be called assisting ministers, liturgists, lectors, or readers, among other titles, and may lead in a wide variety of ways. In some settings the liturgist leads all unison prayers, announcements, other readings, and offers invitations and dedications. Acknowledging your denomination's guidelines, lay readers may take whatever roles the congregation and its pastor negotiate.

scriptural themes time to marinate, soaking up the flavor of the world around us.

## Readers

Because the worship on Sunday morning is the activity of all of God's people, we encourage congregations to include a broad selection of members in planning and leading worship. One way to include various people in the worship leadership is to ask members of the community to read the Scriptures.

Children, youth, and adults can all serve as lectors (readers). Those enlisted to read should be trained to read expressively and audibly. So that readers might be familiar with and understand the texts to be read and so that they can prepare well, they should be given the texts at least a week or two in advance. This preparation might include reading the selected passage aloud for several days prior to the service, perhaps even in the worship space. Readers may also appreciate some background material to help them place the reading in its context and guidance with difficult pronunciations.

Are you interested in training Scripture readers, or starting a lector's group, but don't know where to start? You can find help in G. Robert Jacks's *Getting the Word Across: Speech Communication for Pastors and Lay Leaders.* Thomas Rogers and Seraphim Communications have produced a helpful video training course, called *Turning Ink into Blood.* Aelred Rosser's *Guide for Lectors,* from Liturgy Training Publications, is a relatively brief handbook that could be easily used for discussion and training. (See bibliography.)

Readers might be encouraged to make the assigned readings part of their prayer and devotional life for the week preceding their Sunday. A Scripture reader announces the good news just as the preacher does. Thus, it is appropriate to pray for God's leading as one prepares and proclaims the word.

All but the very smallest churches can recruit and train enough readers so that each person is scheduled only two to three times per year. The first several times a person reads, and thereafter whenever possible, he or she should read the passage aloud for someone who can help the reader speak clearly and expressively. All readers, however experienced, should be encouraged to rehearse. You may want to think of the readers as a team or task force, akin to a choir, that meets periodically to review the upcoming readings and to read for one another. An experienced drama coach, actor, member of Toastmasters, or anyone with good public-speaking skills could be recruited to coach the reading team. Training should cover reading skills, of course, but also logistical considerations, such as where to sit and when to move to the reading stand. With planning, obstacles such as steps and nonadjustable reading desks can be overcome, and older children or people with physical challenges can participate as readers. Reading Scripture is a leadership role that most people can do well when encouraged and trained. At the same time, there are a few people who are difficult to understand or listen to, and these should be gracefully guided into other worship ministries. The task of presenting Scripture is too important to do poorly.

> You may want to think of the readers as a team or task force, akin to a choir, that meets periodically to review the upcoming readings and to read for one another.

# Other Preparation

The preacher also needs to prepare. Preaching well takes time to study the Scriptures and to live with the stories they tell. Preachers also need to know the stories of the people in the congregation and of the larger world. Again, a Bible study can be an important part of the preacher's preparation. Receiving insights from members broadens the preacher's perspective and keeps her or him in touch with the congregation's concerns. The Holy Spirit may guide the preacher through the words of the congregants.

The particular Bible used and the place from which it is read are also worthy of consideration. Some churches have both a lectern and a pulpit, some have only one or the other, and some may have no fixed reading desk, but use a music stand or other improvised support. Some communities may choose to read all Scriptures from one place or the other, or divide readings between the two. Some may even choose to read from neither but rather from the midst of the gathered community. Whatever is decided upon, the location of the Bible and how it is handled have symbolic meaning.

One Bible should be appointed for use in worship. It should be a book of significant size with a sturdy binding that reflects the importance of its contents. At the same time, the Bible is a book to be read from, to be used, not set aside as a decoration and adored from afar. It is best that the Bible not be placed on the communion table. Word and Sacrament have separate symbolic meanings, and the contrast adds depth to each. Rather, the Bible should be kept on the lectern or pulpit from which it is to be read. If placed on the table, it should be moved to a lectern or pulpit for reading. In some congregations, a large and impressive Bible is traditional and appropriate to the formality of worship. In others, a Bible with a well-worn soft-leather cover may be more familiar and valued. In either case, this Bible belongs to the assembly and should be a visible sign of the assembly's worship.

Bible study can be an important part of the preacher's preparation. Receiving insights from members broadens the preacher's perspective and keeps her or him in touch with the congregation's concerns.

The idea of the Bible as the assembly's book, a text shared in community, may have its roots before printing presses brought the Bible into individual hands. The Reformers were eager to have people able to read and interpret the Bible without depending on a hierarchy of clergy. After 500 years of the laity's having personal access to Scripture, the liturgical renewal movement is seeking a balance. In worship we gather as one people to hear and explore together a common word symbolized by a single and familiar book.

It is important to prepare the Bible before the worship event. Readings should be marked clearly, so that the various readers can easily find their passages. If an enlarged photocopy or Braille text is used, these pages should be paper-clipped (or attached with removable tape) in the Bible at the appropriate places. Reading from a folded piece of paper sends a variety of negative messages, including the suggestion that the reader was just handed this sheet and is not ready, or doesn't know how to find the passage in the Bible, or does not care about the rest of the Scriptures. Some churches put the Bible in place before worship begins, while others choose to carry the Bible into the sanctuary as part of a procession. In either case, the Bible, as the book of God's people, is central to the worship space and the life of the congregation.

## For Reflection and Discussion

1. How is the Bible handled in your congregation's worship or in other worship you have attended? Who reads from it? What do your congregation's practices say about worshipers' understanding of the Bible and the value placed on the Bible by the congregation?

2. The suggestions above about the Bible as the assembly's book are intended to help symbolize reading Scripture as a communal activity. What do you think?

# Listening to the Word of God

All the preparation is complete before the service begins, and the people have settled into their seats and are ready to listen. What will they hear?

## Prayer for Illumination

Some churches include a prayer for illumination before hearing God's Word read and proclaimed. In this prayer, the blessing of the Holy Spirit is invoked upon the reading, hearing, and proclamation of the Word, for as Calvin states, "He illumines our minds by the light of his Holy Spirit and opens our hearts for the Word and sacraments to enter in, which would otherwise only strike our ears and appear before our eyes, but not at all affect us within."[3] We ask God's blessing so that in the reading and hearing the word may truly become God's word for the listeners.

The reader of the first reading (which follows immediately) or the preacher may offer this prayer, or the congregation may pray in unison. The prayer might be sung using a chorus such as "Spirit of the Living God," found in many hymnals. A congregation might rotate through a series of prayers, or a new one might be composed for each occasion.

---

A prayer for illumination from the Presbyterian *Book of Common Worship:*

God our helper,
by your Holy Spirit, open our minds,
that as the Scriptures are read
and your Word is proclaimed,
we may be led into your truth
and taught your will,
for the sake of Jesus Christ our Lord. *AMEN.*[4]

---

This invoking prayer follows an appropriate pattern as it calls on the Spirit to be present in the reading, in the proclaiming, and in the listening.

## The Readings

The readings might be preceded by a brief introduction such as, "Our first reading is from the book of Deuteronomy." Announcing the specific verses to be read is usually not necessary when readings are listed in the bulletin, unless people are encouraged to follow along in personal or pew Bibles. Some background information can help listeners prepare to hear. The reader might say, for example, "Our epistle reading is from the first letter of Paul to the Corinthians. Here, Paul writes to the church at Corinth concerning the practice of the Lord's Supper." Care should be taken that introductory material does not become a "mini-sermon." In most situations, the readings speak for themselves with only a simple line or two of introduction.

Readers participate in worship by telling the story of God to the gathered community. "Story" is the key. Ordinarily, the Scriptures are not acted out (although drama or storytelling can be excellent techniques). The goal is to read with expression that brings the stories to life. Excessive dramatic interpretation may call more attention to the reader than to the story. The balance is difficult yet crucial.

*Readers participate in worship by telling the story of God to the gathered community.*

---

*I love reading scripture aloud. To think that God can use me as an instrument through which God's holy Word comes to life is a profoundly thrilling spiritual experience. For years I've tried to instill that same love in my students. I've tried to teach them to believe the most important part of the worship service is the Scripture reading. I've tried to get them to think of the reading as the "gem in the setting of the worship service."*

G. Robert Jacks, *Getting the Word Across*[5]

On any given Sunday, one reader may read all the readings, or various readers may participate. It is good to end each reading or group of readings with a closing in which the reader and congregation claim the passage as the holy Word of God. Often readers end with, "The Word of the Lord" or "The Word of God for the people of God," to which the people respond, "Thanks be to God." Denominational resources offer suggestions. Consistency is important, so that the people come to know their response by heart, but this line should also be printed in the bulletin or projected on a screen so that newcomers are included.

Ordinarily, the *first reading* is from the Old Testament. Many congregations use the term "Hebrew Scriptures" instead of "Old Testament," both to recognize their origins and to guard against the tendency to dismiss the "Old" as superseded by the "New." We are children of Sarah and Abraham, and the stories about God in relationship with God's people throughout time are our stories, too. Through the readings, we hear of the creation and the exodus. We learn from the prophets and the Wisdom writings. We hear of a people, our people, trying to follow in God's way. The Revised Common Lectionary substitutes readings from Acts during the weeks following Easter to remind us of the new history of which we are a part, the history of the church.

A *psalm* is suggested to follow the first reading. Psalms may be read or sung. The singing of psalms was part of the worship life of ancient Judaism, and sung psalms have been part of Christian worship life from the outset. While opinions varied among the Reformers as to the role of musical instruments in worship, all seemed to agree that the singing of psalms was to be included. John Calvin thought that psalms were the only appropriate music for worship.

The psalms appointed for Sundays in the Revised Common Lectionary have often been chosen as responses to the Hebrew Scripture reading rather than

While opinions varied among the Reformers as to the role of musical instruments in worship, all seemed to agree that the singing of psalms was to be included.

Throughout the history of the Reformed tradition, singing the psalms in worship has been important. In some branches of the Reformed tradition, sung psalms have been the only music permitted. John Calvin and other Reformers believed that the singing of the psalms was important because it involved the entire congregation joining in the praises offered. Further, the Psalms are Scripture—the word of God in song form.

as texts to stand alone. The praises and the laments of the psalmists become our praises and laments. Although we do not know how they originally sounded, the psalms were written for singing. They work best as the congregation's response when the psalms are sung by everyone, rather than performed by a choir, though there are wonderful choral settings of psalms. If the choir sings, printing the words encourages the congregation to pray along with the choir. Congregations may sing psalms in several ways. Denominational hymnals are an excellent place to start. Most contain an index of scriptural allusions that includes settings of psalms as well as hymns based on the Psalms. Many newer collections of psalm settings are readily available and contain settings easily accessible by most congregations. Others set psalms to various forms of chant, also known as psalm tones. A few tones or tunes are enough to allow a congregation to sing any psalm that is marked or "pointed" at the places where the chant note changes. Many hymnals, such as the Lutheran, Episcopal, and United Methodist, offer all these options.

Psalms are sung in metrical, responsorial, and other forms. Metrical psalms are either direct quotations from Scripture or close paraphrases set in strophic form to hymnlike tunes. William Kethe's setting of Psalm 100, "All People That on Earth Do Dwell" is sung to the tune named, appropriately enough, "Old Hundredth." Responsorial psalms follow a "call-and-response" pattern between a cantor-leader and that gathered community. A cantor sings the verses of the psalm, and the congregation sings a response after a group of verses. Or the psalm may be divided so that a leader or one side of the congregation reads one verse alternately with the other side.

Communities might want to use the same psalm for a liturgical season. Another option would be to use the appointed psalm for a Sunday with one of several familiar psalm refrains interspersed between lines read or sung by a leader. United Church of Christ (UCC) and United Methodist (UMC) hymnals include these refrains with their pointed psalms. This might be one way to introduce the singing of psalms to a congregation.

The *second reading* usually comes from the letters or epistles in the New Testament. The writings of the developing church are read for instruction and inspiration.

A *hymn, anthem,* or *spiritual song* may be included in response to the readings thus far and as preparation for the Gospel reading to come. The text may restate or interpret one of the Scriptures read or anticipate the Gospel to come. Alternatively, a song may celebrate the gift of the Scriptures as God's word. Yet another appropriate response to the readings is a "praise chorus" or an Alleluia.

In the *Gospel readings,* we experience the living Christ as we hear the stories of Jesus's pre- and post-Easter ministry. In some traditions, people stand for

*Our experience, our perspective, affects what we hear in the text. The Spirit is active in our new experience, stirring up what might be called "new memories of Jesus," new possibilities of the meaning of his life, his words, his death and resurrection. . . . On the other hand, while our experience opens up new dimensions in the story of Jesus, that story as preserved in the biblical texts also challenges and confronts contemporary experience. . . . We cannot simply refashion Jesus in our own image. Rather, the gospels and the history of Jesus limit and focus our retelling of the story.*

Mary Catherine Hilkert, "Naming Grace: A Theology of Proclamation."[6]

One way to help congregations become accustomed to more Scripture readings is to vary the number of people doing each reading. Perhaps a parent and child read the Hebrew Bible (Old Testament) lesson, one other person reads the epistle as if he were Paul preaching, and three people read the Gospel as a dialogue. Perhaps for a liturgical season, we all read the Gospel lesson together, or, as in some churches, alternate verses between reader and congregation. Are there other configurations or traditions that you use or could use in your congregation?

In the Gospel readings, we experience the living Christ as we hear the stories of Jesus's pre- and post-Easter ministry.

the reading of the Gospel to honor the importance of these texts to our Christian faith. In other congregations, members prefer to honor all parts of Scripture in the same way. Local tradition and preferences should guide. Readings from all four Gospels should be included in the sequence of readings over the course of time.

Long historical precedent has established the pattern of readings just described. The flow is toward the Gospel, the central witness to Jesus Christ. Often preachers and leaders of worship revise the order, so that the reading to be preached on is the last one read. When the preacher is also the reader of the last Scripture, he or she is able to talk about and place a distinctive emphasis on the text as it is read. We believe that this factor is not a strong enough reason to change the order. Shuffling the readings overemphasizes the sermon by making the reading of Scripture secondary. When the texts are presented well, listeners are able to remember them well enough to connect them to the sermon.

Protestants tend to place great importance on the sermon. While the Protestant liturgical renewal also honors the sermon, it promotes a sense of balance between liturgy and sermon. The prayers and hymns are more than introduction and conclusion; rather they are the acts of worship of the people of God.

Many congregations are not used to hearing so much Scripture in worship. Some preachers and worship planners include only one or, at most, two readings. Readings are limited because of time, or because not all readings are used directly in the sermon, or—quite frankly—because their presentation is undervalued and ill-prepared, and therefore boring. Including all three readings and the psalm response maintains the breadth of the narrative of Scripture. Even texts that are not preached on have value as texts to be heard. The Holy Spirit speaks with power through the words of Scripture alone.

If for some reason a congregation chooses not to read all the Scriptures each week, care must be taken so that over time readings from the whole of Scripture are included. It is easy to assume that we are reading Scripture to the familiar faces in our congregation each week. The church's mission to share the good news means that we need always to be aware of those who are new and who may not know the Scriptures at all. We should not simplify Scripture for those who are new, but read it fully and clearly. We do not know what story or text will be the one that resonates in a person's heart or transforms a life.

> Including all three readings and the psalm response maintains the breadth of the narrative of Scripture. Even texts that are not preached on have value as texts to be heard.

> The church's mission to share the good news means that we need always to be aware of those who are new and who may not know the Scriptures at all.

## For Reflection and Discussion

1. Should congregations increase the reading of scripture during worship? Why or why not?
2. How can we increase the scriptural literacy of our congregants in worship?
3. Review the suggestions in the sidebar on page 58. Are there other ways to present scripture that will make the text more accessible and interesting?

## The Sermon

After the Bible readings are concluded, the preacher explores their meaning for those gathered today. Through the power of the Holy Spirit, the sermon reveals the ways that the God of the stories of the Hebrew Scriptures is working in the present. Through the Holy Spirit, Jesus the Christ of the New Testament offers good news.

The sermon is one of the greatest challenges as we make worship more participatory. What can the preacher do to discourage listeners from approaching the sermon as an entertainment or lecture, and instead encourage an attitude of engagement and discernment?

The sermon should be simple in structure and accessible to all. Restraining the length of the sermon is one approach to this goal. In most mainline denominations, from 12 to 18 minutes will suffice. Listeners tend to shut down after that. Historical material helps set the stage but should be brief and to the point. The preacher should be able to state the theme in a single sentence. Use stories and illustrations that illumine aspects of the theme to help people remember and to keep interest high. Consider a narrative model for the sermon, a plotline that carries people along from an initial question to a possible solution instead of the old "three points and a poem" model. A sermon style that varies from week to week helps to keep both preacher and listener fresh and engaged.

Most important, the sermon must address the real concerns listeners face. The sermon is an interpretation of Scripture that offers insight into God's will for our lives. A lecture on theological premises or princi-

> Through the power of the Holy Spirit, the sermon reveals the ways that the God of the stories of the Hebrew Scriptures is working in the present. Through the Holy Spirit, Jesus the Christ of the New Testament offers good news.

---

"Liturgical preaching" is a term used to describe preaching that gives careful consideration to the worship service as a whole. Liturgical preaching aims for a unity of sermon with hymns, prayers, and sacraments. Images, themes, moods, and liturgical occasions blend and overlap between the various parts of the service. Such preaching attends to the flow of worship—from Scripture, to sermon, to prayers, and communion—in the construction and delivery of the sermon. A liturgical sermon is one part of a much greater whole. How could liturgical preaching become a part of worship in your congregation?

ples is not a sermon because it is abstract and does not apply theology to life. What Daniel did long ago is a good story but has only passing interest if it doesn't help people now. The goal is to bring the text alive in ways that are meaningful to daily life.

The sermon proclaims and interprets the Scriptures. There are many ways to accomplish this aim other than a monologue. The sermon might take the form of a dialogue between two people, a short drama, a series of songs, a musical, a presentation of artwork on a video, or other creative expression.

The preacher has a responsibility to bring the gospel alive to listeners of all ages. Many congregations of all denominations have few members under age 50 and see their teens leave the church after confirmation. Sermons need to address the concerns of youth and young adults. Preachers may need to make a special effort to identify those concerns. Sermons should use relevant illustrations. Jesus chose images from the lives of his listeners. Potential listeners are important, too. Sermons need to be bold. Jesus never skirted difficult issues, and if the church is to have a moral identity in our pluralistic world, and attract and keep question-filled young adults (and older adults!), we must address the world with conviction. Conviction and condemnation are not the same, of course. We have a great hope to proclaim. Let us never be afraid to declare that hope in word and deed.

For Reflection and Discussion

1. How do you respond to the suggested length for sermons?
2. Should sermons try to include references to and examples that are relevant to youth and children? Why or why not?
3. What ways of responding to the sermon would be most meaningful to you? Which would be most helpful in your congregation?

## Response

Having heard the word of God proclaimed in readings, song, and sermon, the people are invited to respond in faith. Usually communal, this response reaffirms the corporate nature of our worship after the more reflective act of listening to the sermon. Reciting one of the historic creeds of the church, a confessional document, or scriptural passages is an appropriate corporate act of affirmation. People might also be given an opportunity to make or renew their personal commitment to the call of the gospel.

Many congregations sing a hymn or other song that captures the themes of the readings and sermon. The people may gather close together as they celebrate a baptism or confirm young people or commission people for ministry as short-term missionaries or Sunday school teachers. A time of quiet might follow to offer a time for personal response. What is important is that we should actively respond to the Word read and proclaimed. Ultimately, we respond by following in the path of discipleship and receiving the grace offered.

*Offering* our financial gifts in support of the work of the church locally and globally is one way to respond to the ongoing call of Scripture and sermon. It reflects our commitment to the community of faith. We may be stirred to greater generosity or moved to support a special need in addition to our planned offering. The work of God through all the settings of the church goes on whether the preacher inspires a person on any given day. A call to offering announces that the time has come, but it should also remind people of God's call to share with all in need.

The offering is also a time when some congregations include a "mission moment" or other narrative about a supported project. Such an element can be either very distracting or very moving. Great care should be taken here. For congregations that use projected images, a photo montage over simple music may be an effective possibility.

What is important is that we should actively respond to the Word read and proclaimed.

The altar call, a time when people filled with emotion come forward to a team that prays with them and may offer them materials to strengthen their commitment, or even the rite of baptism, is a traditional response to the proclamation of the Word. Other approaches may be more appropriate in your congregation. A range of opportunities should reflect the daily and weekly recommitment and rededication of lives to a path of faith long chosen, as well as the sudden transformation of life after an encounter with God's presence. The community of faith is important to each. Congregational prayers of dedication, a time of silence with a suggested prayer of commitment, or an opportunity to write down one's commitment to be either brought forward or placed in the collection plate—all are appropriate options for weekly renewal. Your congregation may want to prepare a pew card or bulletin insert with options for making a new or renewed commitment to Christ and the church. A personal contact is vital after a sudden transformation. Perhaps one person each week can be a designated prayer partner available for those who wish to make a personal dedication. This contact could be followed by a visit from a pastor or a congregant. How will your congregation respond to new faith found in worship? Do you believe that God can be so deeply experienced in your worship?

Very often, the offering is accompanied by an offertory, a musical presentation by the organ, the choir, another group, or a soloist. As the people are usually passing offering plates or watching for the approach of ushers, the offertory is often not broadly participatory. Too often this routine act of worship is disconnected from the theme of the rest of the service. With attention to the whole of worship, the offertory can connect the Word proclaimed to the acts of love and mercy to which Christ calls us all. A common closing for the offering is the congregation's standing and singing a response such as the Doxology ("Praise God from Whom All Blessings Flow"), or a verse from a hymn such as "We Give Thee but Thine Own," followed by a prayer of dedication spoken by one or by all.

Other offerings may be combined with the primary one. People may bring food-pantry items, or time-and-talent forms, or prayer requests. These may be dedicated separately or along with the financial offering.

# Other Concerns

We have walked through the order of this portion of the worship. Before we move on to the primary response to the Word—the Eucharist (Holy Communion or the Lord's Supper)—several related issues deserve some attention and explanation.

### The Lectionary

A lectionary is a schedule of readings to be used in public worship. Various lectionaries have been used in Jewish and Christian worship for centuries. Many denominations today make use of the Revised Common Lectionary, a schedule of four readings for each Sunday of the year, selected ecumenically, and designed to cover all Gospels and a wide range of other texts over the course of three years. Using the lectionary offers a sense of unity with other Christians near and far, because the RCL is used in many denominations and around the world, so that many people are reading the same Scripture lessons on the same Sunday. The lectionary provides consistency and ensures that the full breadth of Scripture is heard as part of the community's worship.

The predictability of readings allows the community to read and reflect on the Scripture lessons individually or in groups during the week before they are used in worship. Other advantages of the Revised Common Lectionary include the availability of coordinated church-school curricula for all ages and the abundance of sermon and devotional resources based on it, offered in journals, in books, and online.

While some worship leaders are legitimately concerned about whether the Revised Common Lectionary is inclusive enough in its selection of passages, the lectionary does offer a starting place. Pastors and leaders of worship might supplement or substitute various

> While some worship leaders are legitimately concerned about whether the Revised Common Lectionary is inclusive enough in its selection of passages, the lectionary does offer a starting place.

readings to enlarge the breadth of the Scripture read or to examine a particular theme of local relevance.

## For Reflection and Discussion

> Is a lectionary used in your congregation? If so, are there ideas in this book that would enhance your use of all lectionary readings? If not, is it something your congregation should consider? Why or why not?

## Children's Sermon

Readers may notice that no mention has been made of a "children's sermon" or "time with children" thus far. We share the preference of many liturgical scholars and worship leaders that the entire worship event should include all people present as much as possible, regardless of age. By baptism, we are all made one in Christ. Therefore, all baptized believers, of whatever age, have a right to be included in the worship life of the congregation.

If a congregation includes a children's sermon in worship, it might consider evaluating how this element functions in the service and what it is intended to do. One of the principles stated in the beginning is that the patterns of worship shape how we pray and live. There is no better way for children to learn about worship and to know it as a vital and important part of Christian life than by being present and participating in the whole of it. We are not suggesting that children will understand everything that is said, or that everything should be simplified for them. When we consciously attempt to make all of worship more approachable to various ages, our worship is far more inclusive. All of worship will be more vital when the experiences of people of all ages, single and partnered, with children and without, and from a wide

By baptism, we are all made one in Christ. Therefore, all baptized believers, regardless of age, have a right to be included in the worship life of the congregation.

A few congregations have been successful in combining the Scripture readings with the children's sermon in their less formal services. The children come forward, receive a brief introduction to the readings, and then listen before returning to their seats. The presentation of the Scripture readings has changed with the children in mind, but both children and many adults have found the explanations and the more creative presentations of Scripture to be helpful.

range of social and economic settings are reflected in the language of prayers and sermons.

Adults often think that they should be able to worship through their minds alone. They give up the games of childhood for a verbal approach. But people of all ages need a variety of stimuli to gain the greatest experience from worship. Lively, singable songs, color and pictures, other visual expressions of the worship theme, such motions as clapping or raising hands while singing, or walking forward for offerings or communion or baptism all aid in our praise and prayer and engage children and youth in action. A really good children's sermon introduces the day's scriptural themes to both children and adults without making cute objects of the kids. Incorporating similar stories and visual aids in the regular sermon and in other parts of the service can bring the children into all of worship.

Children can contribute regularly to worship in a variety of ways. Some church-school curricula are lectionary based, and children can learn and teach songs, create and offer thematic artwork, and carry appropriate symbols into worship. Pictures used in church school can illustrate worship, bridging the children's experiences from one to the other. Older children can read Scripture, dramatize a biblical story with puppets, or make up a contemporary story or illustration and tell it to the congregation. Too often, children's participation in worship is identified as a special event. One of the authors of this book was a member of a youth choir that almost always participated in

Sunday worship and usually had a response to sing. It may have been a small part, but they knew they were a part of the whole, week after week. This kind of participation takes planning and coordination, but youth and children can contribute and feel important in many ways, whatever the size of the congregation.

## Pew Bibles

Many churches have pew Bibles. For some of us, following along as a passage of Scripture is read is enriching and helps keep our attention on the words. For others, it is isolating or even distracting. Other people find that simply listening together is more communal and allows them to focus on meaning in the text that isn't available in written words alone.

Some congregations print the readings in the bulletin or on an insert. Some bulletin services offer printed lectionary readings. Whether printed texts or pew Bibles are available, they should be of the same translation as the Bible from which the texts are read. (Other translations make for interesting Bible studies, but can be distracting in worship.) If a different version is read, be sure to include that information in the introduction. We encourage active listening, however that is best achieved. Pew Bibles or printed texts address those who listen best as they read and those who have difficulty hearing. People need these options (and enough information to use them, like page numbers of Scripture lessons). We would urge congregations not to pressure people into reading along, however. There are other times and places for people to learn to find passages and to become familiar with the Bible.

For some of us, following along as a passage of Scripture is read is enriching and helps keep our attention on the words. Other people find that simply listening together is more communal and allows them to focus on meaning in the text that isn't available in written words alone.

## Silence

Worship is often filled with words. Silence gives us time to ponder what has happened, to catch up with the flow of worship, to think about what we have heard, and to listen for the whisper of God's spirit in our hearts. Leaders and designers of worship should consider how silence might be integrated into worship. Even brief pauses can create a less rushed pace and let ideas sink in a bit. Longer moments of silence can deepen the impact of words and give us time to absorb and accept the call of Christ upon us.

For example, those who read Scripture tend to be afraid of "dead air" and jump into reading too quickly. It is, in fact, a good idea for readers to anticipate events and to move smoothly into place while the previous element is ending—during the last verse of a hymn, perhaps. Once at the lectern, however, it is good to pause and look up before beginning to read. A pause gives everyone a time to settle in from the last activity: people resume their seats if they have been standing, children decide which lap to sit on, the fluttering of bulletins dies away. Another brief pause after the introduction gives the reader a moment to focus, and the listener time to catch up and absorb what has been said. These intentional pauses are not "dead air," but good timing.

A longer period of silence might be included after each reading. Lent and Advent are more reflective seasons, so they are especially appropriate times to introduce these periods of silence. Some communities include silence following the sermon. Silence was mentioned earlier as appropriate after a prayer of confession to allow each person to confess privately to God. How much silence feels right? Each congregation will need to determine the timing, but we would recommend beginning with about 20 seconds of silence and slowly increasing to one minute. After staying at a minute for a while (a few months), the planning team may want to re-evaluate and determine if more time would be appreciated.

Often when silence is introduced, worshipers feel uncomfortable—a baby cries, papers rustle, someone shuffles her feet, another coughs, some people look

> Worship is often filled with words. Silence gives us time to ponder what has happened, to catch up with the flow of worship, to think about what we have heard, and to listen for the whisper of God's spirit in our hearts.

around. Many wonder what to do. Yet, over time, and with a little guidance, most people become comfortable with times of quiet. They learn what to do: pray, ponder words or phrases just heard, remember joys, experience the community members surrounding and loving one another.

The beauty of silence takes time to be appreciated. People have to settle in and then be quiet. It is so easy to rush that leaders may need to add 20 seconds more than they think necessary in each quiet moment. With a little practice, people will learn to be comfortable with silence and contemplation as one more way to worship.

Song, prayer, offering, and dedication respond to Scripture and sermon and prepare us for the sacramental act of Christ's presence with us and our acceptance of Christ's call upon our lives in the rite of Holy Communion, the topic of the next chapter.

# Chapter 3

# Prayer and Sacrament
*Enacting Our Faith*

So far, we have come together in a living, purposeful community that is open to God's presence. We've worked together with the Spirit and one another to wrestle a blessing from Scripture, to interpret its meaning for each of us as individuals and for our life together as a community of faith. After these acts of worship, we move naturally toward enacting our role as hearers of the word by joining in thanksgiving and in prayer for the world. We move toward being not only hearers but also doers of the word (James 1:22).

It's not that we have been passive up to this point and now suddenly spring into action. We have been active all along: gathering and centering ourselves as a community in relationship with God and each other as we sing, pray, and interpret God's word in Scripture together. Now we are invited, even moved, by all we have experienced to respond to God's reassurance and call. Before we go forth to enact that response in our daily lives, we first enact it in worship: offering prayers and our own lives and resources on the world's behalf, offering thanks, and sharing bread and cup.

In some of our churches, a typical Sunday service concludes with the sermon and a hymn. This order is understandable. The 16th-century Reformers placed a high value on the reading and interpretation of Scripture. They were reacting to centuries in which the

Now we are invited, even moved, by all we have experienced to respond to God's reassurance and call. Before we go forth to enact that response in our daily lives, we first enact it in worship: offering prayers and our own lives and resources on the world's behalf, offering thanks, and sharing bread and cup.

Mass was recited in Latin that people could not fully understand. The Reformers translated the Bible into local languages so that it could be heard and interpreted by all. This emphasis on the sermon has continued to our own day. Earlier we mentioned the frontier worship style that led many congregations to place the sermon near the end of worship. In the early 20th century, scholars studying the Reformation renewed the emphasis on a teaching sermon as the highlight of worship. Alongside this history is another thread that has gained strength in recent years, one that encourages the weekly celebration of communion.

We encourage congregations to move deliberately toward weekly communion. When the sermon is followed by only a hymn and a brief benediction, we are often left to translate our encounter with Scripture into individual action on our own. Too frequently, our encounter with Scripture is forgotten before it can take root, lost as we scramble to get ourselves, and perhaps our families, out the door. The responses to Scripture outlined in the previous chapter allow us to respond and to absorb the message. Communion takes this response further; it enacts and embodies our commitment through physical action.

Fifteen years ago, Daniel Johnson and Charles Hambrick-Stowe asked the United Church of Christ, "What does it mean that, after more than twenty years of being told that a weekly service with both preaching and communion should be the norm, so few congregations have embraced the practice? The sixty-minute worship limit is probably one factor. . . . Another factor slowing the movement to a weekly service of Word and Sacrament may be the predominance of the Baptist and revivalist tradition in American culture today. . . . Finally, there is the oft-heard argument that quarterly or monthly communion emphasizes its specialness, while too-frequent repetition breeds lethargy, not liturgy. But those who participate in weekly (or even daily) communion testify that this is far from the case, that weekly gathering at the table of Christ is the real center of the church and a much-needed nourishment of spirit and community."[1]

Our society is rejecting the purely intellectual approach to belief. Congregations searching for pastors often specify that they want someone who can help them connect faith and life in ways that are more concrete and meaningful. In keeping with the worldwide ecumenical convergence of the past half-century, together with the books of worship that have been published by our denominations in the last few decades, we encourage worship that recovers the ancient balance between listening for God and enacting our faith—between Word and Table.

What if, having opened ourselves to God's grace and the work of the Spirit in worship, we simply could not go back to our lives as if nothing had happened? What if we took the next step together—enacting a just, peaceful, and grace-drenched world in worship—and so prepared ourselves to go and work for that world in the rest of our lives? As we walk through this chapter, we attempt to take these tantalizing possibilities seriously. We will be using a model of weekly prayers of the people and communion here with the belief that our comments will apply to monthly or quarterly celebrations as well.

> We encourage worship that recovers the ancient balance between listening for God and enacting our faith—between Word and Table.

> What if we took the next step together—enacting a just, peaceful, and grace-drenched world in worship—and so prepared ourselves to go and work for that world in the rest of our lives?

## Preparing Ourselves

Even before Sunday morning, our preparation for full participation in the prayers of the people can begin. In our private prayer and in prayers shared with family or small groups, we come to know those things that are most on our hearts, concerns we might choose to share with our faith community in prayer. If Sunday morning is the only time in the week that we will pause for any length to pray, we may be tempted to turn inside ourselves, and to use the occasion for private prayer. But if our daily lives are filled with prayer, times of personal meditation and private piety, then we are less likely to be preoccupied, trying to cram

If our daily lives are filled with prayer, times of personal meditation and private piety, then we are less likely to be preoccupied, trying to cram a week's worth of joys and concerns into this one moment.

a week's worth of joys and concerns into this one moment. We will be freed to join more fully in the congregation's prayerful task on behalf of the world. We will be able to pray as a community, open to one another and to God, blending our particular concerns and thanksgivings with the prayers of others.

It is the same with communion. Just as the Eucharist itself (from the Greek *eucharisto,* meaning "thanksgiving") is about giving thanks, so we can prepare ourselves for communion by giving thanks regularly throughout the week. The interdependence between daily private prayers of thanksgiving and the public prayer of the church is stronger than many of us recognize. If prayers of gratitude to God are not woven into the fabric of our daily lives, if we do not give thanks as individuals and as families from time to time throughout our days, then our participation in communion is likely to seem relatively empty and disconnected from life (especially if our celebrations of communion are also rare!). But if communion can become the guiding example of our thankful meals at home, then our practice of giving thanks for home meals can prepare us for greater depths of thanksgiving at the sacramental meal.

## Planning for Prayer and Sacrament

Those who will lead communion must also prepare carefully. The increasing focus on the sermon as the central activity of worship in our denominations has produced ministers who may spend a good deal of time preparing to preach, but little or no time prepar-

*Remembering that we worship a God who casts down the mighty and scatters the proud, presiders should be willing to evaluate their skills [at leading the Eucharist] periodically by means of videotape and consultation.[2]*
Richard McCarron, *The Eucharistic Prayer at Sunday Mass*

ing to preside. In order to lead well—that is, to lead in such a way that all may participate easily and actively—ministers and lay leaders need to practice, to think through the movement of communion, and to memorize particular parts, if not all of the communion prayer. Also, like all who participate in communion, presiders will be able to participate more deeply if they are grounded in a life of prayerful gratitude. For congregations to experience depth of meaning in the communion service, they will need to expect, and allow time for, such pastoral preparation.

The simple food around which the congregation will gather should be lovingly prepared, despite the pressures of efficiency and convenience. Bread that is delicious and wholesome, firm enough to handle, but easy for all to eat, will be most likely to engage us and encourage our full participation. Wafers, hard unleavened squares, or soft, tiny cubes present a "thin" symbolism, disconnected from real life. A full loaf of good bread has a "thick" symbolism, an expression of real life and a connection with all the meals that sustain us. It resists the thoughtless hurry of efficiency and speaks clearly of nourishment, of renewed strength. Preferably, the bread is baked by a diverse group of congregation members, even in the church kitchen. A good, simple loaf presented with minimal cutting is experienced fully as a common loaf from which we all share and of which we all can claim to be a part. An alternative, if crumbs in the cup are a concern, is a pita bread or other flexible flatbread.

> The simple food around which the congregation will gather should be lovingly prepared, despite the pressures of efficiency and convenience.

---

*Baptismal immersion is certainly not universally practiced. Neither is "communion in both kinds," the whole community eating from one loaf and drinking from one cup. . . . does the community both eat and drink? Is there one loaf, one cup? For many communities these remain important, even revolutionary, questions. As with all matters of liturgical practice, these questions are to be approached with wisdom and love, but they must be raised.[3]*

Gordon Lathrop, *Holy Things*

---

The cup, whether juice or wine or both are made available, will better carry its rich symbolism if it is prepared so that its depth and richness as a source of life are clear. Because the liquid, and not its container, is most important to us, chalices and pitchers are best if not overly ornate, but simple and attractive. Clear glass containers allow everyone (and not just those who preside) to see the liquid inside, even from far away.

A shared common cup has a long history and origins in early Christian practice. Even more important, a common cup allows us to enact our unity in Christ; we share the same cup, the same covenant, and the same blessing. Whether we drink from a common cup (which is the practice in many churches, and which carries minimal health risk if wine is used), or use intinction (the act of dipping a piece of bread in the cup), we physically demonstrate our participation in that common blessing, just as tearing a piece of bread from a common loaf demonstrates our participation in the one body of Christ.

Many of us have received miniature, single-sip cups and small squares of bread passed in trays in our pews or distributed at a communion rail. This practice does have its own positive symbolic values. The bread and cup come to us where we are, just as God's grace does. Passing trays along the pew allows us to serve one another, rather than receiving only from those who are chosen to lead. Still, this practice has often allowed us to slide toward passivity. We have often come to see ourselves as recipients waiting to be served, rather than as people who gather to eat and rejoice together. Even when we have all waited to eat and drink the elements at the same moment, our individual servings

> A common cup allows us to enact our unity in Christ; we share the same cup, the same covenant, and the same blessing.

---

*Then he took a cup, and after giving thanks, he gave it to them, and all of them drank from it.*

Mark 14:23

Perhaps your congregation isn't ready to move to a single loaf and cup yet. Are there ways to pass trays and regain the corporate nature of the rite? If members of your congregation don't currently speak to one another in passing the elements, this is a good place to start. "The body of Christ," we can say, or "the cup of salvation." "Amen." We can highlight the communal meaning in the prayers and preaching. We can sing together as the trays are passed, or speak or sing a response after receiving each element and when all have been served. (One church we know sings a verse to a specially written song before eating and before drinking and then after all have communed.) Even if you are still using trays, you might experiment for a season with moving in procession to the table to be served.

have tended to drive us toward private piety, toward personal time with God, rather than toward the communal experience of God's presence among us that is so crucial for corporate worship.

Some congregations, including many Methodists, have had the practice of gathering in groups at a communion rail and kneeling to receive the elements. Communion is served to each person, usually using small cups, and the group is dismissed together. Variations on this model exist as well. This practice does encourage movement during communion and is quite communal. People are gathered before the table of the Lord, as we are called to do. Kneeling emphasizes reverence, an attitude often missing from casual contemporary worship. Some congregants feel that they are kneeling before the minister, however, so a misplaced reverence can occur. In addition, this practice is often the norm in sanctuaries where the table is elevated and set against a wall. Perhaps if done with care, bringing the table and kneeling rail into the midst of the assembly could be a powerful model for the sacrament.

In other settings, people move forward to receive the elements while standing, but a kneeling rail is available for personal prayer. This custom acknowledges the mix of private and corporate meaning in the communion service.

A table that is accessible to all, including those in wheelchairs, will communicate more than whatever words we might pile up in sermons and prayers about our equality in Christ.

For those congregations that move forward to or gather around the table (something we would encourage), preparation may also include work to ensure that it is possible for everyone to approach. A table that is accessible to all, including those in wheelchairs, will communicate more than whatever words we might pile up in sermons and prayers about our equality in Christ.

Many of our sanctuaries were designed so that the communion table would evoke the Holy of Holies in the Jerusalem Temple: an inner sanctum that could be approached only by those who are qualified, and even then only cautiously. Consequently, in many sanctuaries the communion table is raised or in some way cordoned off, usually placed against a wall so that it can be approached but not surrounded. Certainly the visibility of the table is a concern that shouldn't be neglected, and the table should be given enough space of its own to signal its sacred purpose. Still, if the primary model for our meals in worship is the ministry of Jesus, then we should all be able to come to the table. Congregations will likely be amazed at how a sanctuary where the communion table is truly in the midst of the people will increase their participation in and ownership of the meal. Against the grain of our contemporary culture of entertainment, and in contrast to the architecture of the theatrical stage with its rows of spectators, the table that stands in our midst invites us to gather round as Christ's disciples.

---

*The holy table should be the most noble, the most beautifully designed and constructed table the community can provide. It is the common table of the assembly, a symbol of the Lord. . . . It stands free, approachable from every side, capable of being encircled. Its symbolic function, of course, is rendered negligible when there are other [tables] in sight. The liturgical space has room for but one.*

*Environment and Art in Catholic Worship*[4]

---

When we come to communion having prepared ourselves to be habitually grateful people, and having prepared our meal to be both communal and rich with meaning, we are much more likely to find ourselves being more fully engaged in the meal. We are also more likely to be drawn into a communal experience of Christ, who has promised to be not just in our private thoughts but there in the midst of us when we gather.

## At Worship: Prayer and Sacrament

Again we move from planning to a discussion of the elements of the prayer-and-sacrament movement of worship. Elements of this part of worship might include:

Prayers of the People
Invitation
Preparation of the Table
Communion Prayer (or Great Thanksgiving)
Opening Litany
Thanks for God's Work
Response: Holy, Holy, Holy (Sanctus)
Thanks for Christ
Words of Institution: Telling the Story (Anamnesis)
Blessing of the Gifts (Epiclesis)
Sharing of Bread and Cup
Final Prayer of Thanksgiving

### Prayers of the People

After the sermon is over, a period of quiet reflection has passed, a response has been spoken or sung, and the offering has been taken, we begin responding to God's call to incarnate the good news in our own flesh. Although denominational worship orders vary here, we often begin by praying as people of God on behalf of the world. This is something that we do as

Prayers that are truly *of the people* encourage us all to participate; to bring our own cares and joys along with the cares of the world, to open ourselves to God's unmediated presence, and to enter into the constant, universal prayer of the community of saints.

*Unless we understand that the word is stronger than the will; unless we know how to approach a word with all the joy, the hope or the grief we own, prayer will hardly come to pass. The words must not fall off our lips like dead leaves in the autumn. They must rise like birds out of the heart into the vast expanse of eternity.*[5]

Abraham Joshua Heschel, *Man's Quest for God*

a community. We do not need anyone, clergy or lay leader, to pray in our stead. Prayer leaders assist us in the joyful task that we do as a community.

Prayers that are truly *of the people* encourage us all to participate; to bring our own cares and joys along with the cares of the world, to open ourselves to God's unmediated presence, and to enter into the constant, universal prayer of the community of saints. Congregational responses during intercessory prayer may help to give us all an active role. Spaces can also be created within the prayer for people to offer their own prayers aloud. A petition spoken by the leader might invite prayers for people affected by violence, for example, and people can speak aloud the names of people and places in need of such prayer. The leader closes each petition with a cue such as "God, in your grace," and the people respond, "Hear our prayer."

Some people are uncomfortable offering prayers themselves and would rather tell their prayer concerns to a prayer leader. We mentioned earlier that concerns could be gathered verbally at the beginning of worship. In some congregations, prayer concerns are gathered just before the prayer by the minister, who then repeats them in prayer. In others, prayer cards are collected for incorporation in a prayer. We would encourage people to offer their own prayers, but if a minister is praying, it should not be necessary to repeat fully a prayer request heard just before the prayer. A reference will remind all of the need and better incorporate the unspoken concerns of others.

A pastoral prayer that focuses on the sermon topic does not, by itself, constitute the Prayers of the People.

A pastoral prayer that focuses on the sermon topic does not, by itself, constitute the Prayers of the People.

Many such prayers are just reiterations of the sermon and probably should be eliminated entirely. Others assume that people are ready to commit themselves to the specific course of action outlined in the sermon and may not express the hearts of the people. A pastoral prayer, if it is believed necessary, may be the conclusion to the sermon and may be followed by a hymn and the offering, Some pastors mix the two, but we urge ministers to let petitions for peace and healing, for the church and the world, to have their own regular part of every worship, with or without communion. That does not mean that the sermon theme will not affect the way the petitions are shaped. And it can be good for leaders to make prayers specific enough to pull people a bit beyond their comfort zone.

The people most often pray in words. They may also pray through a gesture or action. By coming forward to light a candle or to place a written prayer in a basket or to tie a ribbon onto a Christmas tree, we are able to engage both mind and body in prayer. Each of these types of prayer might be concluded with a unison prayer, collecting the prayers of the people into one voice.

> By coming forward to light a candle or to place a written prayer in a basket or to tie a ribbon onto a Christmas tree, we are able to engage both mind and body in prayer.

## Eucharist or Holy Communion

After praying for the world, the minister may move to the table to begin the rite of communion. In most cases, some preparation will be needed.

Preparation at the table varies with the table appointments. In some settings, elements are present

---

Throughout this discussion we use the term "table" to refer to the communion table. Others use the term "altar." For many people these terms are interchangeable. Using "table" reminds us of Jesus's practice of dining with outcasts and sinners, and this is our preferred model for the Eucharist. The term "altar" recalls the traditional and complex imagery of sacrifice, which is also a part of our Christian heritage.

When the bread and cup are brought to the table by members of the congregation, we can see clearly that the meal belongs to all of us as a group table. We are reminded that these gifts come from the people for the people.

but covered and must be uncovered and cloths laid aside. When bread and wine are brought forward, they are placed on the table. Other traditions include a hand-washing ritual at this point, with a bowl of water and towels used by all servers before moving to the table or handling bread or cup. This is usually more symbolic than hygienic, but some have added a small container of waterless hand cleaner in this germ-conscious age. When servers who have washed their hands break bread and give it to communicants, people are freed to take and eat without worry of contamination. When the bread and cup are brought to the table by members of the congregation, we can see clearly that the meal belongs to all of us as a group table. We are reminded that these gifts come from the people for the people. Adding such an action requires practice and a level of serious attentiveness appropriate to the worship service.

The elements may be brought forward as part of the general offering or during the singing of a communion song. They do not magically appear. God gives to us grain and fruit. Human hands convert them to bread and wine, living symbols and carriers of great meaning as they are broken and poured out in Christ's name and memory.

In many churches a vital link has been lost between the presentation of the communion elements and the presentation of our gifts for the ministries of the church and for people in need. Just as we come to the table with gifts of our own wealth, so also we bring the fruits of the earth and human labor in bread and cup. The two are connected, for in both cases the practice of returning gifts to God prevents us from simply using up everything on earth without giving anything back. Both practices help us to work toward a balance of giving and receiving that is necessary to sustain life on earth. These gifts also remind us that God is the true owner of all that we might claim.

When laypeople "set the table" by placing the elements on the table themselves rather than handing them over to the clergy, we may better understand communion as a meal prepared and shared by all. Of course, if clergy are the only ones at the table during the sacrament that follows, then it may appear that laypeople have simply set the table for the more important people who follow them. Many congregations now invite servers and assisting ministers to stand around the table during the communion prayer as community representatives.

As the table is prepared, we are all continuing to prepare ourselves as well, since communion, like the rest of worship, is something that we will all do together. In our posture, our attentiveness, and our attitudes, we prepare to come to the table as participants rather than as spectators. We also prepare to open ourselves to Christ's presence in *us,* for if Christ is present anywhere in the communion service, he is present in and among those who gather in his name.

> We also prepare to open ourselves to Christ's presence in *us,* for if Christ is present anywhere in the communion service, he is present in and among those who gather in his name.

### The Invitation

With the words of invitation, the service of communion begins. Through the invitation we are called into the household of God, called to give thanks, and called to join in Jesus's ministry of living out God's

---

*Hospitality and Communion.* We would urge congregations to be aware of the way the invitation and other materials address newcomers. Will they know whether they are welcome to participate and what to do? Clear instructions in the bulletin are important. A member may also invite a newcomer to sit with her and offer cues to guide the newcomer throughout the service, especially during communion. The more complex the pattern of worship, the more important having a guide can be. Having someone reach out in a friendly and helpful way can make the sacrament an experience of communion for a newcomer.

realm in our own flesh. We are called to gather about Christ's table and to join in the meal to which he has invited us. We come as guests at the banquet, ready to join in, with bodies, hearts, and minds.

The invitation is the first act of worship that is directly part of the communion liturgy. Whether a brief sentence or a longer statement, it invites people to come to the table of Christ. In many congregations, this statement is worded to help people decide whether to participate in the sacrament. It may mention membership in the denomination or baptism in Christ's church, or it may open the table to all who desire to follow Christ. In many cases, a description of the process for taking communion follows.

In some orders of worship, the invitation precedes a prayer of confession, the pardon, the passing of the peace, and the offering. The United Methodist orders for Word and Table use this pattern, for example. In others, the confession comes earlier, and the invitation leads directly to the opening litany, or to the offering, which includes bringing forward the bread and wine.

## The Great Thanksgiving

With the beginning of the Great Thanksgiving prayer, we enter the main body of the Eucharist. Most of our communion prayers follow a similar structure. Together, we offer thanks for all of God's acts in history. We may remember the creation of the world, the freeing of the Hebrew people from slavery, or the wisdom of kings and prophets. Often this part of the prayer includes the Sanctus, an ancient response beginning "Holy, Holy, Holy, Lord God of Hosts." Our grateful remembrance recalls our own faith heritage and thus reminds us who we are. We go on then to offer particular thanks for the gift of Jesus Christ, praising God for raising him from the dead and saving God's people. In some prayers, the response to this portion is the acclamation "Christ has died. Christ is risen. Christ will come again."

The prayer continues with the story of Jesus and the first communion meal (the words of institution) and with a petition to the Holy Spirit (called the *Epiclesis*) to bless the assembly and the prepared bread and wine so that it may transform our lives to be one people led by Christ. The people may respond with a rousing "Amen."

We do all of this together—as brothers and sisters in Christ. Because all are equal before God in this meal, and because God's power over evil and despair is declared, the prayer challenges the secular powers that seem to control our lives. The communion prayer helps to make room for us to imagine justice and peace even where none seems possible. Most of all, it prepares us for the meal, awakening us to Christ's presence and the Spirit's activity in our midst.

For centuries, and in many congregations today, churchgoers have considered the communion prayer to be something uttered solely by ministers. We listen in on the prayer (or parts of it) and chime in for a few sung or spoken sentences. Here we often fall into the twin traps of clericalism and consumerism: clergy and other leaders "perform" the prayer while the rest of us wait passively to be entertained and then served.

If we are all participants, however, then both the prayer itself and our roles in it may be quite different. We may decide to adapt our communion prayers to increase congregational participation by having some parts of the communion prayer read in unison or

> The communion prayer helps to make room for us to imagine justice and peace even where none seems possible. Most of all, it prepares us for the meal, awakening us to Christ's presence and the Spirit's activity in our midst.

*The very remembering of the mighty deeds of God disrupts the way things are now as much as the events named turned [our] ancestors' world on end then. The very remembering undoes the powers that be and trounces the thought that what is, is all there is.*
Richard McCarron, *The Eucharistic Prayer at Sunday Mass*[6]

responsively as litanies. However, since some people
find that the necessity to concentrate on our next line
detracts from the meaning, it is equally important that
some parts of the prayer (such as the acclamations) remain constant from season to season and from year to
year. This constancy allows all of us to commit some
parts of the prayer to memory. Then the whole congregation, and not just its ministers, has some ownership of the communion prayer. The traditional pattern, found in many hymnals and other resources, is a
prayer framework with constant cues and responses,
but with room for seasonal or thematic portions that
fit between. The assembly comes to know the cues
and responses by heart but can hear or speak a fresh
thanksgiving for God's work in the world.

If the whole congregation is going to claim ownership of the liturgy (the "work of the people," after all)
and the worshipers are to become active participants,
then we will need to rise to the occasion as the prayer
begins. Through our posture and attention, we will
want to engage ourselves fully in what we are doing.
We may also want to think seriously about how we
participate physically in the prayer in ways that are
connecting rather than isolating.

In many communities it is common for those who
are able to stand for the majority of the prayer. These
might adopt the ancient *orans* posture, standing
with eyes and arms open and palms up. The minister
could model the posture for all. She or he may raise
or extend the arms during the *Epiclesis* (the part of
the prayer asking for the Spirit to bless the elements);
then the people might extend their arms as well. Such
physical participation may feel awkward or contrived
at first, but if such actions are chosen and explained
with care, they are likely to increase our sense that we
are all doing this together.

We may also want to increase our connection with
those who preside and with each other. We may want
to see each other's faces and not just the backs of each

We may want to see each
other's faces and not just
the backs of each other's
heads. We may want those
who preside to look us in
the eye, and not just at the
prayer text.

other's heads, for example, or we may want to make the passing of the peace of Christ part of our communion service. We may want those who preside to look us in the eye, and not just at the prayer text. Of course, this eye contact requires that the presiders have prepared, as we mentioned above, by memorizing most or all of the communion text.

Memorizing the text can limit the minister's ability to keep the service fresh and appropriate for the context, since it is difficult to memorize a new communion prayer each week. But knowing the prayer by heart does allow the presider to interact with the congregation more freely, communicating with eyes, arms, facial expression, and posture. Another option for the minister is to memorize the structure of the prayer and the cues and responses, and then pray it naturally, adding and adapting as she or he prays. One may lose some refinement of language that comes with a carefully composed text, but the connection to the assembly is strengthened. We then move toward the banquet in which we find ourselves looking across the table at our sisters and brothers in Christ, eager to share as we celebrate the meal together.

## Sharing of the Elements

After the prayer, we move to share the food with each other. We talked earlier about the use of a common loaf and a common cup as a sign of our sharing with one another. If we are going to intentionally engage in communal and participatory worship, we may also want to carefully consider who serves whom and how. How we "do" the meal matters because it helps to prepare us for how we are going to live as people of faith in the world.

What are we "learning by doing" when only those in authority serve the meal? When they stand above us on a step or raised platform to serve us? When only males serve (in stark contrast to most of the meals

If we are going to intentionally engage in communal and participatory worship, we may also want to carefully consider who serves whom and how. How we "do" the meal matters because it helps to prepare us for how we are going to live as people of faith in the world.

of ordinary life)? When those who serve physically touch (without asking) those who receive but not vice-versa? When some individuals are named aloud as they receive while others are not? Some congregations may want to consider formats in which people serve each other, whether in circles or in lines. Using a diverse group of lay servers that changes from week to week may symbolize that broad participation as well. We may also want to ask that the ministers be served neither first nor last, but somewhere in the middle as part of the congregation. In these ways, all serve as Christ did, and all receive from the hand of Christ.

Many congregations are now coming forward to communion stations to be served and then moving back to their seats. When asked, most people express a feeling of community as the congregation moves together. A clear and smooth flow of people helps dispel the sense of standing in a line. Although this practice has been called "drive-by communion," the experience of the community as one body can be very rich when the servers speak the words of distribution with attention to each person, the movement is calm, and the serving is accompanied by appropriate music or singing.

---

Communion is serious, but need not be solemn. Here is an example of a final thanksgiving from the former Zaire (now called Democratic Republic of the Congo) that requires no printed words:

| | |
|---|---|
| God, may we glorify your name! | Yes! |
| Your name! | Yes! |
| Very honorable! | Yes! |
| Living God! | Yes! |
| Son! | Yes! |
| Holy Spirit! | Yes! |
| May we glorify it! | Yes! |
| Today! | Yes! |
| Tomorrow! | Yes! |
| Forever and ever! | Yes![7] |

### Final Thanksgiving

Finally, when we have made sure that everyone who desires to be fed has partaken, and, in some congregations after an *Agnus Dei* ("Lamb of God, who takes away the sins of the world, have mercy on us") has been sung, we join in a prayer of thanks for the meal we have shared. This prayer provides us with one more opportunity to address God together. It also helps us begin to move from worship to the world, from our labor alongside God in worship to our labor with God in all times and places. Again, a unison prayer makes sense, for we need no intermediary. Or it may be a responsive prayer, full of excitement and joy, that is fitting for the great celebration of God's gift of love we have enjoyed.

# Worship without Communion

As we have made clear, we believe that the celebration of the Eucharist should be a weekly event, as it was for the early church. Yet we recognize that many congregations participate in monthly or less frequent Communion. On days without communion, the service often goes directly from the Prayers of the People to the final hymn. This pattern may leave us without a time of shared thanksgiving for the whole of God's saving work.

One place in the service for an act of thanks is at the offering. A longer offertory dedication prayer could offer thanks to God for the gifts of creation and history, for Christ and Spirit. Reference to the loaf and cup is also appropriate as a reminder of the sacrament of renewal and unity.

Another way to celebrate on a day without Holy Communion is with a separate act of gratitude. People could light candles or place prayers of gratitude written on slips of paper in a basket or on a banner or recite a litany of thanks with a sung response. A litany could begin with the same opening lines as the Great Thanksgiving: "Lift up your hearts! We lift them in thanks and praise."

The goal of these options is to ensure that every worship service includes a significant element of remembrance and thanksgiving. It also has the effect of creating a regular space for the Eucharist in the pattern of worship in the hope that weekly communion will become an important and meaningful part of every worship. Whatever our act of thanksgiving, it should inspire a mood of celebration and make us ready to be sent forth in service to Christ.

## For Reflection and Discussion

1. Remember an experience of Communion that was special for you. What did you feel? What made it special?
2. Based on the authors' ideas and your personal experiences, reflect on the practices of Communion you have known. How do they differ from the recommendations of the authors? How are they similar?
3. What are the benefits of using the same worship practice each week versus the benefits of using a range of practices? How important or disturbing is variety to you?
4. The Eucharist is an event rich in symbolism and meaning. What is your primary understanding of this sacrament?
5. What meanings of the Eucharist are expressed in your congregation's practices? What images catch your attention? How is God addressed? What parts of the Christian story are remembered?
6. Imagine participating in a Communion service you would think of as "ideal." How would the Communion elements be distributed? What would the physical setting look like? What do

you imagine your experience to be like? What parts of this ideal celebration could be used in your congregation?

7. If your congregation celebrates communion less than weekly, what do think might be the benefits of and barriers to more frequent celebration?

8. Would you recommend weekly communion to the congregation? If not, why not? If so, how would you introduce the practice?

9. On pages 89–90, the authors propose that an Act of Thanksgiving be a part of every service. Discuss the presence of thanksgiving in weekly worship. In what ways can worship help your congregation become a more thankful people?

# Chapter 4

# Sending Forth

The final movement in the worship service takes us from gathered assembly back to our daily lives. The interlude of worship is nearly over. As worship planners and leaders, we might think that the work is done, but we must leave as with as much care as we entered, and so we must prepare.

When well planned, the final moments of worship help us make the transition back to the tasks of work and family and service by collecting all that has taken place in worship and affirming the importance of what is to come. We ease this transition by carefully selecting a final hymn or song and selecting or writing words of sending and benediction. In some traditions, the end of worship is also the time for announcements of events and concerns in congregational life.

The interlude of worship is nearly over. We might think that the work is done, but we must leave as with as much care as we entered, and so we must prepare.

The combination of assurance and challenge that we often experience at the close of worship has deep roots in Christian tradition and identity. Jesus's final speech at the end of Matthew's gospel, for example, includes "Go therefore and make disciples of all nations," as well as "Be not afraid, for I am with you" (Matt 28:19-20). When we sing a hymn that both stirs and sends us, when we begin talking and thinking about the various ministries of the church, when we hear both a charge and a blessing (or, in some free church traditions, a benediction that includes elements of both), the mixture helps us to solidify who we are and what we are about in the world.

What is the experience of people in your congregation? Do they feel sent, commissioned, even challenged at the end of worship to go and work for God's realm on earth? Do they feel affirmed, Spirit-filled, and blessed for the tasks ahead? The feedback that you get from church members might help you begin thinking about the kind of transition (or lack of one) that happens in your church at the end of Sunday worship and what new possibilities you might imagine.

Making announcements at this time makes sense, because these announcements turn our thoughts to the tasks of shared life and ministry that go on outside worship. As when announcements come at the beginning, the way they are selected, labeled, and introduced can make the difference between a disruption and a natural part of the flow. Whether serious or lighthearted, good announcements offer concrete ways to continue enacting our faith in our everyday lives.

## Final Hymn

The last hymn is often rousing and inspiring, reminding people of God's love and desire for a world of faith, justice, and peace, and calling them to action on God's behalf. Pay attention to the mood of worshipers after using various hymns, and choose most often those that encourage strong, positive responses to Christ's call to service in keeping with the theme of the day. Many good final hymns are not prayers addressed to God as much as they are statements of dedication. It can be quite effective to have people turn away from the central focus on pulpit and table and face one another as they sing, and remain turned for the blessing to follow. Where people are in pews with a central aisle, turning to the center encourages interaction and unity.

# Commissioning

The words that close the service should be brief and direct. Although it is not universally used, a commissioning or charge often occurs *before* the benediction. Using images from Scripture and sermon or communion, a commissioning reminds us of our call to serve and declares that we are empowered by the Spirit to act in Christ's name. This is a commissioning of the people for their work, a declaration of mission. It should be simple and brief, but it should not shy away from challenging people. One of the most important models from Scripture is the Great Commission: "Go therefore and make disciples of all nations, baptizing them in the name of the Father and of the Son and of the Holy Spirit, and teaching them to obey everything that I have commanded you" (Matt. 28:19-20).

# Benediction

The benediction is a blessing offered to all. It is usually trinitarian in form. Some traditions use biblical benedictions, which are familiar to all. Or one may be

---

Blessings may be sung, whether in the well-loved words of "God Be With You Till We Meet Again," or in a newer, gender-shifting song such as this one:

May the blessing of God go before you.
May Her grace and peace abound.
May Her Spirit live within you.
May Her love wrap you 'round.
May Her blessing remain with you always.
May you walk on holy ground.

Words and Music by Miriam Therese Winter. Copyright © 1987 Medical Mission Sisters. All rights reserved. Used by permission.

---

taken from a cultural tradition, such as a Celtic blessing, or written for the occasion.

Whatever text one uses, it should be prepared and preferably memorized so that it can be addressed directly to the assembly. It is appropriate for the congregation to respond to a benediction spoken by one person with at least an "Amen." Other brief responses would also be appropriate. A well-known benediction could be spoken or sung by the congregation, perhaps with members turned to face one another rather than all facing in one direction. Again, the benediction is better memorized than read from the bulletin, but do not neglect to print it there for newcomers. A communal sung "Amen" is also a well-loved conclusion in many congregations.

## Dismissal

Tradition offers us a biblical dismissal in the Song of Simeon, the Nunc Dimittis. This dismissal is sung or spoken in some congregations or on specific occasions. In others, the minister may dismiss the assembly with such words as "Go in peace; serve the Lord." (In the *Lutheran Book of Worship*, the congregation responds, "Thanks be to God.") These may be simply the final words of the benediction rather than identified as a separate act of worship.

## Postlude

Whatever kind of postlude is planned, honor the overall flow of the service so that the assembly moves out into the world transformed and blessed and strengthened for all that lies ahead

In most settings a postlude or other music is played after the benediction. Out of a belief that getting up and leaving during the postlude is disrespectful, some congregations ask that the people sit and listen. We would urge reconsideration of this practice, which makes the postlude a mini-concert, and which usually does not flow naturally from the rest of the service. Music can be for walking and marching, for going out as well as for listening. A reprise of the last hymn, or a brief fanfare that keeps people on their feet may serve the purpose far better. Whatever kind of postlude is planned, maintain the overall flow of the service so that the assembly moves out into the world transformed and blessed and strengthened for all that lies ahead. Weak or disconnected endings such as post-benediction announcements or a wait for the postlude to end can blur the message from all that has gone before. It is a paradox of faith and life that endings are beginnings, and beginnings are endings. As the service of worship ends, the service of life in and for the world begins, and the preparation for the next gathering begins as well.

## An Epilogue

This short book has covered a lot of territory in a fairly limited way. Many other resources will help you continue to explore specific topics. We have chosen not to suggest many beyond your denominational hymnal and book of worship because these are excellent places to start and because we have tried to address ourselves to a set of principles. We hope that this reflection about worship is applicable across a wide range of theological and stylistic approaches.

Some of what we have said probably seems familiar to readers whose congregations have adopted the patterns of the recent hymnals and books of worship. To others, we may seem to be proposing a "traditional" model as opposed to a "contemporary" one. In our culture, tradition tends to have a short memory. Most of the resources from the liturgical renewal movement are 20 years old or less, an age that may seem ancient to some. Still, adopting a new or different form or pattern is not enough to create vital and meaningful worship, whether it is rooted in history

We urge you to return to the principles presented in this book's introduction. Discuss them in your worship committees, explore their implications, test our recommendations against them, and throw out what does not fit.

and scholarship or in the current music fads. We urge you to return to the principles presented in this book's introduction. Discuss them in your worship committees, explore their implications, test our recommendations against them, and throw out what does not fit.

Lutheran liturgical theologian Gordon Lathrop asserts that Christian worship is about the juxtaposition in the assembly of bath and table, prayers and the Word, together with concern for the poor.[1] Community, baptism, Scripture and proclamation, Eucharist, and mission are the center of Christian practice. Vital worship practice can make these, and the God who is present in them, alive and central in the lives of all who participate.

## For Reflection and Discussion

1. How could the worshiping congregation best be sent out into the world?
2. What is your experience of the close of worship? What would enhance that experience?
3. Review the principles of worship below. Do you agree with them? Why or why not?

> Worship is the core of the church's life.
> Worship is the work of the people of God.
> Christianity is a communal faith.
> Worship does not take us away from life but changes how we live.
> The patterns of worship shape how we pray and how we live.

4. Where are the principles best reflected in your congregation's worship now?
5. Which principles and concerns raised in the book would you most like to see addressed?
6. How might the principles be modified to better fit your congregation?

7. Imagine an ideal worship service that reflects the principles and ideas from this book that are most significant for you. What would it be like? How would you feel as a participant in that worship event?

8. Could your ideal be implemented on a weekly basis in your congregation? Why or why not?

9. How does the service:

> invite participation and foster an experience of God's presence?
> help build the community of faith?
> affect the lives of the participants?
> develop patterns of worship that strengthen faith?

# Appendix A

# Leader's Guide

This guide is intended to help groups study *The Work of the People* to reflect on their congregation's regular Sunday worship service. It will help your group (1) broaden its understanding of the elements of worship and how together they create a coherent and integrated worship service and (2) prepare for full participation in worship. It will better equip those involved in planning worship for their task.

This study uses an appreciative approach. This means we have shaped the questions to elicit what is good about worship rather than criticism of current practice. We believe that by building on the positive, we can enhance and revitalize worship and our communities of faith. During the study, criticisms may arise. These are important and should be acknowledged and discussed if others share the concerns. Following such a discussion with a question such as "What would be a way to improve this situation?" can return the group to a positive approach.

This guide does not assume the leader has any special knowledge beyond a familiarity with the book and the congregation's own worship practice. We hope leaders will join in the discussions and participate in the group work along with other study participants.

# Possible Formats

Using the questions for discussion and reflection in the text plus the activities suggested below, a study group could engage in a detailed study of worship in ten sessions of about one hour each. A suggested outline is presented below. The sessions build on one another. Other study approaches may better suit your situation. You may want to focus on the principles or on a specific portion of worship. A worship-planning group may want to begin a year's work with a retreat and cover most of the material over two days.

## A Ten-Session Study

1. Introduction to the Study/Principle 1
2. Principle 2
3. Principle 3
4. Principles 4 and 5
5. Gathering
6. The Word
7. Holy Communion/Response to the Word (up to the ideal communion service)
8. Holy Communion/Response to the Word 2/ Sending Forth
9. Putting it All Together
10. Closing Worship

## Adaptations

- Five sessions: The study may be completed in five two-hour sessions by combining two sessions into one, with a short break in the middle. In the last session, delay the break until just before the worship time.
- Retreat: The study may also be adapted to a two-day retreat for a worship-planning team. Sessions would be regrouped into four two- to three-hour blocks as follows:

Sessions 1, 2, and 3
Sessions 4, 5, and 6
Sessions 7 and 8, using optional discussions
Sessions 9 and 10, with a break before worship

A planning team would need time during the retreat to prepare for closing worship, but some work would need to be done before the retreat to provide resources for liturgy and environmental art suitable to the selected theme.

# Materials

Each participant should have a copy of *The Work of the People* to read at home and use during the study sessions. Provide as needed:

- Nametags
- Pens or pencils and paper
- Bibles

In addition, the following materials will be helpful while studying several sections.

- Copies of past worship bulletins
- Hymnals
- Your denomination's book of worship, if you use one in addition to the hymnal, which may have background material or additional Sunday services of interest to the group
- Copies of your congregation's mission statement for use with Principle 1

# Preparing the Space

- Make a poster with the principles of worship on it, allowing room for additions or modifications.

- Arrange seating to accommodate conversation in groups of three or four and as a full group. Tables will be very helpful. Be sure everyone can hear and see the leader and other participants.
- Set up a space to post newsprint or freezer paper. (Use water-based markers on newsprint or freezer paper to prevent markers bleeding through to walls.)
- Include a piano or keyboard or other instrument (and someone to play, of course) to help lead singing.

## Guidelines for Study Groups

Study groups larger than five or six will benefit from breaking into groups of three or four for part of each session. Questions that ask for participants to share personal experiences or that analyze written materials are best discussed in smaller groups. Recommendations that arise in small groups should be reported back to the larger group.

Keep track of all suggestions and ideas on sheets of newsprint. These are valuable contributions to the community's worship and the basis for the review sessions. If the study group is not regularly involved in worship planning, its ideas should be made available to worship planners, along with a copy of the book. In addition, some of the suggestions may be incorporated in the study group's closing worship.

If there is time and talent, opening each session with singing can help prepare the group for their work. Choose a hymn or song that relates to the topic. A couple of verses of most songs are adequate. Close every session with prayer for the participants and for the worship of the congregation. A brief prayer could be said in unison and repeated each time. Most participants will have learned it by the third or fourth time, enabling people to stand or sit in a circle with hands joined if that is comfortable for the group.

At the beginning of the study, the group leader may want to prepare an introduction to set out the intentions and structure of the study. Be sure to welcome all the participants. Explain that the goal of this study is not to plan a worship service, but to learn about the elements of worship and how they together create a coherent and integrated worship service, and to prepare for full participation in worship. Include the specific interests of your congregation that led to beginning the study.

Encourage participants to make notes of questions or concerns that arise as they read. Take time at the beginning of each session to discuss these questions. In some cases, these may raise more important topics for the group than the reflection questions. At the same time, some members may feel that the session is incomplete if the study questions are not addressed. Balance and flexibility in both leaders and participants make for a productive and helpful study process.

The reflection questions that precede the Principles on page 7 can be used as an icebreaker in the first session. Ask people to talk with one other person, then have each person briefly report on their partner's response.

## Suggestions to Enhance the Study

Principle 2: Worship is the work of the people of God.

- Since increasing active participation in worship is a key goal of this book, ask the large group to discuss ways to build on their experience of times when everyone has seemed engaged. Make a list of these ideas and post it at least through the discussion of the principles.

- If your congregation is considering ways to attract and incorporate new people, you may want to discuss the following: How could our worship begin to reflect the social and cultural makeup of the church's immediate neighbors? People who are new to Christian worship practice? Friends and colleagues who do not attend any church? The people who visit the food pantry? (These groups may overlap! Modify the questions to suit your outreach needs.)

Principle 3: Christianity is a communal faith.

A Bible study may be helpful in the discussion of this principle. Select passages from the list below so that each group of three or four has two verses to study. Be sure that each person has a Bible available. More than one group can use each passage, but in a different combination. Ask groups to reflect on this guiding question: what does the Bible tell you about what kind of community the church is called to be?

Deuteronomy 6:4–9
Deuteronomy 26:16–19
Matthew 13:31–33
Matthew 18:20
John 21:15–19
Acts 4:32–27; 16:40
Romans 12:3–8
1 Corinthians 12:12–22
Ephesians 2:19–22
1 Peter 2:9–10

After 12 to 15 minutes, bring the whole group back together to report their findings. Ask, "How is this biblical idea of Christian community expressed in our congregation's worship?"

Principle 4: Worship does not take us away from life but changes how we live.

Principle 5: The patterns of worship shape how we pray and how we live.

The questions in these sections are intended to help people think about the difference regular worship makes in their daily lives. People who have been worshiping all their lives may not have clear examples of personal change or how worship has shaped them because like all regular practices worship affects us gradually, often without our awareness.

If people find it difficult to answer the questions as stated, redirect the questions by exploring how people respond to the temptations to hopelessness or cynicism or excessive self-centeredness or greed or any other non-Christian action. Has something they have come to believe or some value expressed in worship caused them to make choices different from those of friends or family who do not participate in worship?

Chapter 1: Gathering

- During the discussion, write all suggestions for worship modifications on newsprint sheets. The whole group can refer to the list in the final review session.
- After the study is complete, pass on the accumulated ideas to the congregation's worship planners.

Chapter 2: The Service of the Word

- Before discussing the questions at the end of the section "The Lectionary," pass around copies of a lectionary. These are available in some hymnals, many sermon aids, and in several online resources such as Vanderbilt Divinity Library's website http://divinity.lib .vanderbilt.edu/lectionary/. The Consultation on Common Texts' official guide, *The Revised Common Lectionary,* is available from Abingdon Press and describes the history of the lectionary and its goals and lists the passages for both weekly readings and special days for the three-year cycle. If your congregation is not well acquainted with the lectionary, print or photocopy a portion of one for distribution to each group.

- Ask people to compare the readings for several Sundays or other occasions in the three-year cycle. The weeks following Epiphany, for example, demonstrate that most of the Gospel readings for each year come from a single Gospel. The readings for Ordinary time (Proper 9 and following) illustrate the options available, including sequential readings through a single book. Note that the lectionary is designed to create weekly themes and at some times of the year to provide semi-continuous readings.

- Invite the group to compare and contrast alternatives to lectionary use: (1) choosing themes for worship first and then finding scripture to suit the theme; (2) reading continuously through books of the Bible (*lectio continua*)—which might result in a in a sermon series on Romans, for example; (3) inviting the pastor to choose selections based on the pastor's sense of the congregation's needs (or, occasionally, based on the pastor's favorite sermon topics).

## Option

Groups might prefer to discuss altar calls (see the sidebar on page 63). People may have transforming moments at any time in worship, but after the sermon is a traditional place for such a response.

- How can the congregation make room for or encourage a whole-hearted commitment to Christ as a response to the word proclaimed in sermon and worship?
- In small groups, discuss the questions in the sidebar. (1) How will your congregation respond to new faith found in worship? (2) Do you believe God can be so deeply experienced in your worship?
- It may be appropriate to end the session with a song of commitment.

## Putting It All Together: Review

After looking in detail at all the elements of worship and the ideas that underlie them, look again at the whole and explore ways to introduce the ideas the study group has gathered in your congregation.

### Preparation

- Provide copies of the congregation's current worship order.
- Post the principles sheet.
- Post all the worship ideas from the previous sessions.

### Discussion

- After small groups discuss questions 1 through 4 at the end of "Final Thoughts," gather as a large group and report on their conversation.
- Invite the group to create a consensus statement of principles for worship in your congregation. This is not the setting for a vote. Be sure every group's suggestions are weighed

and discussed. Adjust until all are willing to agree or until there is a clear majority statement. If consensus does not develop, post the alternate ideas alongside the majority ones.

- After small groups discuss questions 5 through 7, ask each small group to share key ideas from its discussion with the whole group.

Option 1: Ask the large group to choose two or three ideas they would like to see included in your congregation's worship.

Option 2: Ask each small group to present its ideal service to the large group. Ask each group to turn in its plan for a service to your worship-planning team. (If this study group is the worship-planning team, plan a time to discuss how each of the services could be implemented.)

## Concluding Worship Service

If the study group is large enough, close with a full worship service with Holy Communion (about 45 minutes) planned by and for study members. Smaller groups may want to ask one or two people to plan a briefer closing worship. In either case, the worship should reflect the group's ideas and priorities.

- Ask for four or five volunteers to serve as a planning team, or invite specific people with particular gifts and enthusiasm for the task. (In most traditions, someone authorized by the denomination or congregation will be needed to preside for communion, so the planners might need to invite a clergyperson to work with them.)

- Provide the team with the accumulated ideas from the discussions, although not all can or should be incorporated in one service. Unity and flow from one element to another are as important as trying out many ideas.
- The team might select a theme or use the next Sunday's lectionary readings.
- Someone should prepare a five-minute homily/reflection on the theme of the selected readings.
- The team may recruit others of the group to serve as readers or musicians, to provide appropriate environmental art, or to serve in other capacities.

# Denominational Worship Resources

## Listed by Denominational Abbreviation and Year of Publication

| | | | | |
|---|---|---|---|---|
| Christian Reformed Church | CRC | | PCUSA | Presbyterian Church USA |
| Disciples of Christ | DOC | | RCA | Reformed Church of America* |
| Episcopal Church USA | ECUSA | | UCC | United Church of Christ |
| Evangelical Lutheran Church in America | ELCA | | UMC | United Methodist Church |

| Element of the Worship Service | CRC 1987 | DOC 1997 | ECUSA 1979 | ELCA 2006 | PCUSA 1983 | UCC 1986 | UMC 1992 |
|---|---|---|---|---|---|---|---|
| Gathering | p. 972 | pp. 6–7, 11–12, 237–293 | pp. 323–325, 355–357 | pp. 92, 94–102 | pp. 48–59 | pp. 35, 58–59, 110–111, 119–120, 525–529 | pp. 13–15, 16–22, 33, 41–42 |
| Confession & Assurance | pp. 972–973, 978–979, 983–984 | pp. 306–326 | pp. 330–332, 359–360 | pp. 94–96 | pp. 52–57, 87–89 | pp. 36–38, 63–64, 100–101, 530–534 | pp. 20–21, 25–26, 35, 44–45 |
| Passing of the Peace | | pp. 426–427 | pp. 332, 360 | p. 106 | p. 57 | pp. 38, 64–65, 102, 116 | pp. 25–26, 35, 46 |
| Prayer for Illumination | p. 973 | pp. 7, 12, 383–384 | p. 325 | | pp. 60, 90–91 | pp. 40, 61, 104, 114 | pp. 22, 34 |
| Readings | p. 973 | pp. 7–8, 12 | pp. 325–357 | pp. 102–103 | pp. 61–62 | pp. 19–27, 40–41, 61, 104–105, 114–115, 122 | pp. 13–15, 22–23, 34, 42–43 |
| Sermon | p. 973 | pp. 8, 12 | pp. 326, 358 | p. 103 | p. 62 | pp. 41, 62, 105, 115–124 | pp. 13–15, 23, 34, 43 |
| Prayers of the People | p. 973 | pp. 13, 337–361 | pp. 328–330, 359, 383–393 | pp. 105–106 | pp. 65–66, 99–124 | pp. 41, 62, 105–106, 115, 122–125 | pp. 13–15, 24–25, 34–35, 43–44 |
| Offering | p. 973 | pp. 9, 13, 389–404 | p. 333 | p. 106 | pp. 67–68, 79–80 | pp. 42–43, 65–66, 107, 116, 123 | pp. 13–15, 26–27, 36, 46 |
| Eucharist | pp. 973–975, 979–982, 984–987 | pp. 9–10, 13–14, 404–425 | pp. 333–339, 361–365 | pp. 106–114 | pp. 67–77, 125–158 | pp. 44–52, 68–74, 74–75 | pp. 13–15, 27–31, 36–39, 46–50 |
| Sending | p. 975 | pp. 10, 14, 427–464 | pp. 339–340, 366 | pp. 114–115 | pp. 82–83, 159–161 | pp. 53–54, 75–76, 108, 116–117, 125–126 | pp. 13–15, 31–32, 39, 50 |

*View on denominational Web site at www.rca.org.

# Annotated Bibliography
## of Worship Resources

Christian Reformed Church in North America. *Psalter Hymnal*. Grand Rapids, MI: CRC Publications, 1987.

> The *Psalter Hymnal* is the official book of worship of the Christian Reformed Church in North America. Published in 1987, *Psalter Hymnal* includes "the psalms, Bible songs, hymns, ecumenical creeds, doctrinal standards, and liturgical forms." Building on the traditional publications of the denomination, the 1987 *Psalter Hymnal* not only includes the historic liturgies of the Christian Reformed Church but also includes contemporary orders and texts. A small selection of texts are included for the various parts of the worship service.

Christian Church (Disciples of Christ). *Chalice Worship*. Eds. Colbert S. Cartwright and O. I. Cricket Harrison. St. Louis: Chalice Press, 1997.

> The publication of this worship resource by the Christian Church (Disciples of Christ) paralleled the adoptions of the denomination's *Chalice Hymnal,* also in 1997. *Chalice Worship* serves as a guide to congregations for planning services of Word and Table. Faithful to the Disciples of Christ tradition, it offers many suggestions for congregations and pastors accustomed to great autonomy in designing worship

services. The worship resources section found toward the back of the book offers options for prayers of confession, illumination, intercession, and eucharistic liturgies and prayers. The introductory material "The Lord's Day Service among Disciples Congregations" honors particular Disciples of Christ traditions while also taking note of the Disciples' commitment to Christian unity.

Episcopal Church (USA). *The Book of Common Prayer*. New York: Seabury Press, 1979. Long title: *The Book of Common Prayer and Administration of the Sacraments and Other Rites and Ceremonies of the Church: Together with the Psalter or Psalms of David According to the Use of the Episcopal Church.*

At the denomination's General Convention of 1789, the convention established a *Book of Common Prayer* for the churches and acknowledged that in the course of time it might be the responsibility of future churches to alter, abridge, enlarge or amend it. The 1979 version did just that, updating the beloved *Book of Common Prayer* in ways faithful to its origins for a new generation. This book contains a schedule of lectionary and Psalter readings, services of morning and evening prayer, Sunday collects in both traditional and contemporary versions, and the texts of Holy Eucharist Rites I and II as well as liturgies for other rites.

Evangelical Lutheran Church in America. *Evangelical Lutheran Worship*. Minneapolis: Augsburg Fortress Press, 2006.

The ELCA has published a new hymnal and worship book, *Evangelical Lutheran Worship*, which is commended to the churches for use and will effectively replace the prior *Lutheran Book of Worship*. Further information on worship is available on the denomination's Web site, www.elca.org/worship, including a summary of the liturgical-review process undertaken by the denomination that has resulted in the publication of *Evangelical Lutheran Worship*. In addition, a list of hymns and background documents on liturgical music and the use of Scripture in the language of prayer and worship are provided.

Presbyterian Church (USA) and Cumberland Presbyterian Church. *Book of Common Worship*. Louisville: Westminster John Knox, 1993.

Developed jointly by the Presbyterian Church (USA) and the Cumberland Presbyterian Church, the *Book of Common Worship* was published in 1993. The resource contains complete orders and texts for worship on the Lord's Day as well as liturgical resources for seasons and holy days of the liturgical year. Eight Prayers of the People and 24 Great Thanksgiving prayers are included. The resource includes materials for baptism/initiation, daily prayer, marriage, funerals, ministry with the sick, as well as a complete Psalter, calendars, and lectionaries.

Reformed Church in America. www.rca.org/worship. The Reformed Church in America conducted a denominational survey of worship practices and attitudes in 2004. The results of the survey are available at the denomination's Web site. Also available in either Rich Text Format or as PDFs are a service for the Lord's Day, which includes the Lord's Supper, and two Lord's Day Preparation Services that include material up to the celebration of the Lord's Supper. At the Web site one can also find seasonal worship materials, the Revised Common Lectionary, special liturgies, and articles about beliefs on the sacraments and about theology and the place of music in worship. Pastors and worship leaders are encouraged to browse and download resources.

United Church of Christ Office for Church Life and Leadership. *Book of Worship, United Church of Christ.* New York: UCC Office for Church Life and Leadership, 1986.

> The publication of the UCC *Book of Worship* in 1986 was a response to the denomination's 1977 General Synod resolution to produce a book of worship for the UCC using inclusive language. The result is a book faithful to the various denominational strands that united to form the UCC. The book is also faithful to ecumenical conversations regarding worship. Pastors and worship leaders find a variety of services of Word and Table and services of the Word, as well as many options for prayers and guidelines for praying extemporaneously, either in the prayers of the people or at the eucharistic table. The Services of Word and Sacrament I and II are sensitive to the discussions about historical patterns of Eucharistic prayer that were taking place at the time of the book's publication. The UCC recently conducted a denomination-wide worship survey, leading to the publication and periodic distribution of additional worship resources to congregations. Some of these materials can be found at the denomination's website, www.ucc.org.

United Methodist Church. *United Methodist Book of Worship.* Nashville: Abingdon, 1992.

> The *United Methodist Book of Worship* contains the official worship resources of the United Methodist Church. The first section of the book, "The Basic Pattern of Worship," establishes the order of worship for Sunday worship. Ordinary and seasonal resources for the various acts of worship follow. Nineteen Great

Thanksgiving prayers are included for Eucharistic celebrations.

# Notes

Introduction, Approaching Worship

1. James White, *Protestant Worship: Traditions in Transition* (Louisville: Westminster John Knox, 1989).

2. From the hymn "We Limit Not the Truth of God," text by George Rawson, 1853; based on words of the Rev. John Robinson to the Pilgrim Community, 1620. United Church of Christ Office for Church Life and Leadership, *The New Century Hymnal* (Cleveland: Pilgrim Press, 1995), 316.

3. Jane Rogers Vann, *Gathered Before God: Worship-Centered Church Renewal* (Louisville: Westminster John Knox, 2004).

4. Second Vatican Council, *Constitution on the Sacred Liturgy* (1962), paragraph 14.

5. Gerhard Kittel and Gerhard Friedrich, eds., *Theological Dictionary of the New Testament* (Grand Rapids, MI: Eerdmans, 1964), vol. 4.

6. Abraham Joshua Heschel, *Man's Quest for God: Studies in Prayer and Symbolism* (New York: Scribner's, 1954).

7. Don Saliers, *Worship as Theology: Foretaste of Glory Divine* (Nashville: Abingdon, 1994).

Chapter I, Gathering

1. Robert Hurd, "A More Organic Opening: Ritual Music and the New Gathering Rite," *Worship* vol. 72, no. 4 (July 1998): 290–291.

2. United Church of Christ, *Book of Worship of the United Church of Christ* (New York: UCC Office of Church Life and Leadership, 1986), 15.

3. For an excellent discussion of existential limits and the way worship helps us to address them, see Jerome W. Berryman, *Godly Play: A Way of Religious Education* (San Francisco: HarperSanFrancisco, 1991).

4. James White, *Introduction to Christian Worship*, 3rd ed. (Nashville: Abingdon, 2000), 49.

5. Gabe Huck, *Sunday Mass Five Years from Now* (Chicago: Liturgy Training Publications, 1989), 129.

6. Selecting music for worship requires some careful judgments, especially when choosing from the Contemporary Christian Music (CCM) so widely available. Terry Bockland McLean's book *New Harmonies: Choosing Contemporary Music for Worship* (Herndon, VA: Alban Institute, 1998) contains helpful advice and tools adaptable to any congregation.

7. Text copyright © 2004, Marcia McFee. Permission is granted for congregations to incorporate this text into their worship at will. McFee's Web site is www.marciamcfee.com.

8. Aidan Kavanagh, *Elements of Rite: A Handbook of Liturgical Style* (New York: Pueblo Publishing, 1982).

9. Huck, *Sunday Mass*, 130.

10. Gertrude Mueller Nelson, "Christian Formation of Children: The Role of Ritual and Celebration," in *Liturgy and Spirituality in Context*, Xavier John Seubert, ed., (Collegeville, MN: Liturgical Press, 1990).

11. The Church of the Province of New Zealand, *New Zealand Prayer Book, He Karakia Mihinare O Aotearoa: The Anglican Church in Aotearoa, New Zealand, and Polynesia*, rev. ed. (San Francisco: HarperSanFrancisco, 1997).

## Chapter 2, The Service of the Word

1. Marjorie Hewitt Suchocki, *The Whispered Word: A Theology of Preaching* (St. Louis: Chalice Press, 1999), 27.

2. Thomas Driver, *Liberating Rites: Understanding the Transforming Power of Ritual* (Boulder, CO: Westview Press, 1998).

3. John Calvin. *Institutes of the Christian Religion*, IV, xiv, 8.

4. Presbyterian Church (USA), *Book of Common Worship* (Louisville: Westminster John Knox, 1993), 90.

5. G. Robert Jacks and Gordon D. Fee, *Getting the Word Across: Speech Communication for Pastors and Lay Leaders* (Grand Rapids, MI: Eerdmans, 1995).

6. Mary Catherine Hilkert, "Naming Grace: A Theology of Proclamation," *Worship* vol. 60, no. 5 (September 1986) 446–447.

## Chapter 3, Prayer and Sacrament

1. Daniel L. Johnson and Charles E. Hambrick-Stowe, *Theology and Identity: Traditions, Movements, and Polity in the United Church of Christ* (New York: Pilgrim Press, 1990), 95–96.

2. Richard McCarron, *The Eucharistic Prayer at Sunday Mass* (Chicago: Liturgical Training Press, 1997), 104.

3. Gordon Lathrop, *Holy Things: A Liturgical Theology* (Minneapolis: Augsburg, 1998).

4. *Environment and Art in Catholic Worship* (Chicago: Liturgy Training Publications, 1993), nos. 71–73.

5. Heschel, *Man's Quest for God.*

6. McCarron, *The Eucharistic Prayer at Sunday Mass,* 13.

7. Ibid., 46.

## Chapter 4, Sending Forth

1. Lathrop. *Holy Things,* 94.

# Bibliography

Berryman, Jerome. *Godly Play: A Way of Religious Education*, 1st ed. San Francisco: HarperSanFrancisco, 1991.

Calvin, John. *Institutes of the Christian Religion*. The Calvin New Translations. Edinburgh: Printed for the Calvin Translation Society, 1845.

Church of the Province of New Zealand. *A New Zealand Prayer Book = He Karakia Mihinare O Aotearoa: The Anglican Church in Aotearoa, New Zealand, and Polynesia*. San Francisco: HarperSanFrancisco, 1997.

"The Constitution on the Sacred Liturgy" (1962) in *The Liturgy Documents: A Parish Resource*, 3rd ed. Chicago: Liturgy Training Publications, 1991.

Driver, Tom F. *Liberating Rites: Understanding the Transforming Power of Ritual*. Boulder, CO: Westview Press, 1998.

Heschel, Abraham Joshua. *Man's Quest for God: Studies in Prayer and Symbolism*. New York: Scribner's, 1954.

Hilkert, Mary Catherine. "Naming Grace: A Theology of Proclamation." *Worship*, vol. 60.5 (1986): 434–449.

Huck, Gabe. *Sunday Mass Five Years from Now*. Chicago: Liturgical Training Publications, 1989.

Hurd, Robert. "A More Organic Opening: Ritual Music and the New Gathering Rite." *Worship*, vol. 72.4 (1998): 290–315.

Jacks, G. Robert. *Getting the Word Across: Speech Communication for Pastors and Lay Leaders*. Grand Rapids: Eerdmans, 1995.

Johnson, Daniel L., and Charles Hambrick-Stowe. *Theology and Identity: Traditions, Movements, and Polity in the United Church of Christ.* New York: Pilgrim Press, 1990.

Kavanagh, Aidan. *Elements of Rite: A Handbook of Liturgical Style.* New York: Pueblo Publishing, 1982.

Kittel, Gerhard, Gerhard Friedrich, and Geoffrey William Bromiley, eds. *Theological Dictionary of the New Testament.* 10 vols. Grand Rapids: Eerdmans, 1964.

Lathrop, Gordon W. *Holy Things: A Liturgical Theology.* 1st paperback ed. Minneapolis: Fortress, 1998.

McCarron, Richard. *The Eucharistic Prayer at Sunday Mass.* Chicago: Liturgical Training Publications, 1997.

McLean, Terri Bocklund. *New Harmonies: Choosing Contemporary Music for Worship.* Herndon, VA: Alban Institute, 1998.

National Conference of Catholic Bishops. Bishops' Committee on the Liturgy. *Environment and Art in Catholic Worship.* Washington: National Conference of Catholic Bishops, 1978.

Nelson, Gertrude Mueller. "Christian Formation of Children: The Role of Ritual and Celebration." *Liturgy and Spirituality in Context.* Xavier John Seubert, ed. Collegeville, Minn.: Liturgical Press, 1990.

Presbyterian Church (USA). *Book of Common Worship.* Louisville: Westminster John Knox, 1993.

Richard, Lucien, O.M.I. *Living the Hospitality of God.* Mahwah, N.J.: Paulist Press, 2000.

Rogers, Thomas. *Turning Ink into Blood.* DVD or VHS. St. Paul, Minn.: Seraphim Communications, Inc.

Rosser, Aelred, O.S.B. *Guide for Lectors.* Basics of Ministry. Chicago: Liturgical Training Publications, 1998.

Saliers, Don E. *Worship as Theology: Foretaste of Glory Divine.* Nashville: Abingdon, 1994.

Suchocki, Marjorie Hewitt. *The Whispered Word: A Theology of Preaching.* St. Louis: Chalice Press, 1999.

United Church of Christ Office for Church Life and Leadership. *Book of Worship: United Church of Christ.*

New York: United Church of Christ Office of Church
Life and Leadership, 1986.

————. *The New Century Hymnal*. Accompanist ed.
Cleveland: Pilgrim Press, 1995.

Vann, Jane Rogers. *Gathered before God: Worship-
Centered Church Renewal,* 1st ed. Louisville: Westminster John Knox, 2004.

White, James F. *Protestant Worship: Traditions in Transition,* 1st ed. Louisville: Westminster John Knox, 1989.

————. *Introduction to Christian Worship*. 3rd ed., rev.
and expanded. Nashville: Abingdon, 2000.